BRITAIN'S BEST ARCHITECTURE

BRITAIN'S BEST ARCHITECTURE

EDITED BY GARY TAKLE

WITH TEXT BY EMMA PEACOCK

Think Publishing Australia

Think Publishing Australia
ABN 97 131 984 128
PO Box 448,
South Morang, Victoria 3752
Australia
Telephone: +61 3 9404 5579
info@thinkpublishing.com.au
www.thinkpublishing.com.au

ISBN 978-0-9871356-6-7

Editor: Gary Takle
Writer: Emma Peacock
with contributions by Jade de Souza
and Corey Thomas

Graphic Design: Tristan Wilson and Jonathan Takle

Front cover photograph: Architecture:m, *Regent Road*
Photography by Andrew Haslam

Back cover photographs:
Left: David Mikhail Architects, *Terrace*
Photography by Tim Crocker
Top Right: Gregory Phillips Architects, *Berkshire*
Photography by Darren Chung
Bottom Right: Waugh Thistleton Architects, *Furzey Hall Farm*
Photography by Will Pryce

Designer: Inglis Badrashi Loddo
Project: Queen Square
Photographer: David Grandorge

Contents

Designer: Gregory Phillips Architects
Project: Berkshire
Photographer: Darren Chung

Designer: Edgley Design
Project: Tower House
Photographer: Jake Edgley

Designer: John Pardey Architects
Project: Watson House
Photographer: James Morris

Designer: Liddicoat & Goldhill
Project: The Shadow House
Photographer: Tom Gildon

Designer: Nicolas Tye Architects
Project: Dovecote Barn
Photographer: Nerida Howard

Designer: Waugh Thistleton Architects
Project: Furzey Hall Farm
Photographer: Will Pryce

FARNBOROUGH

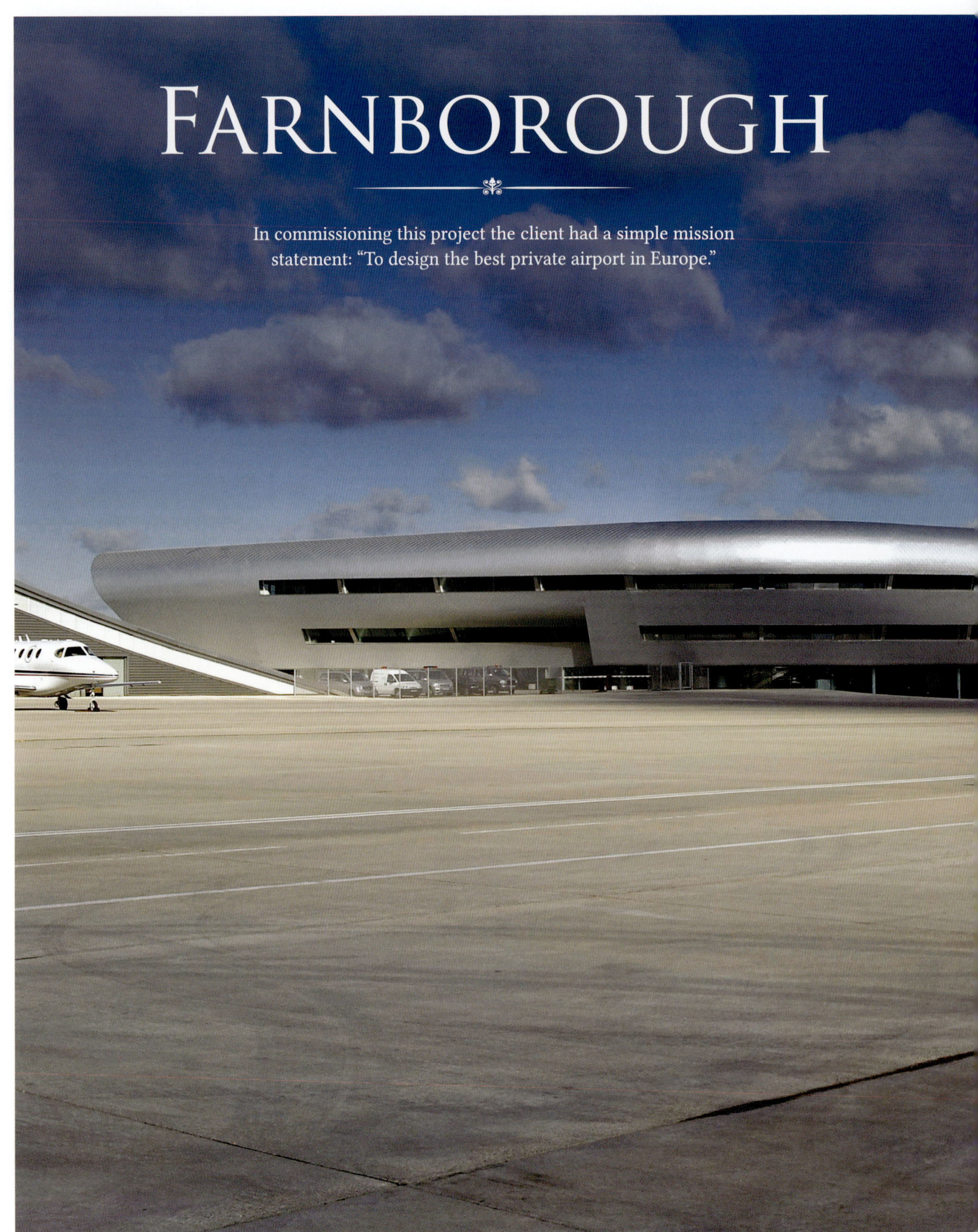

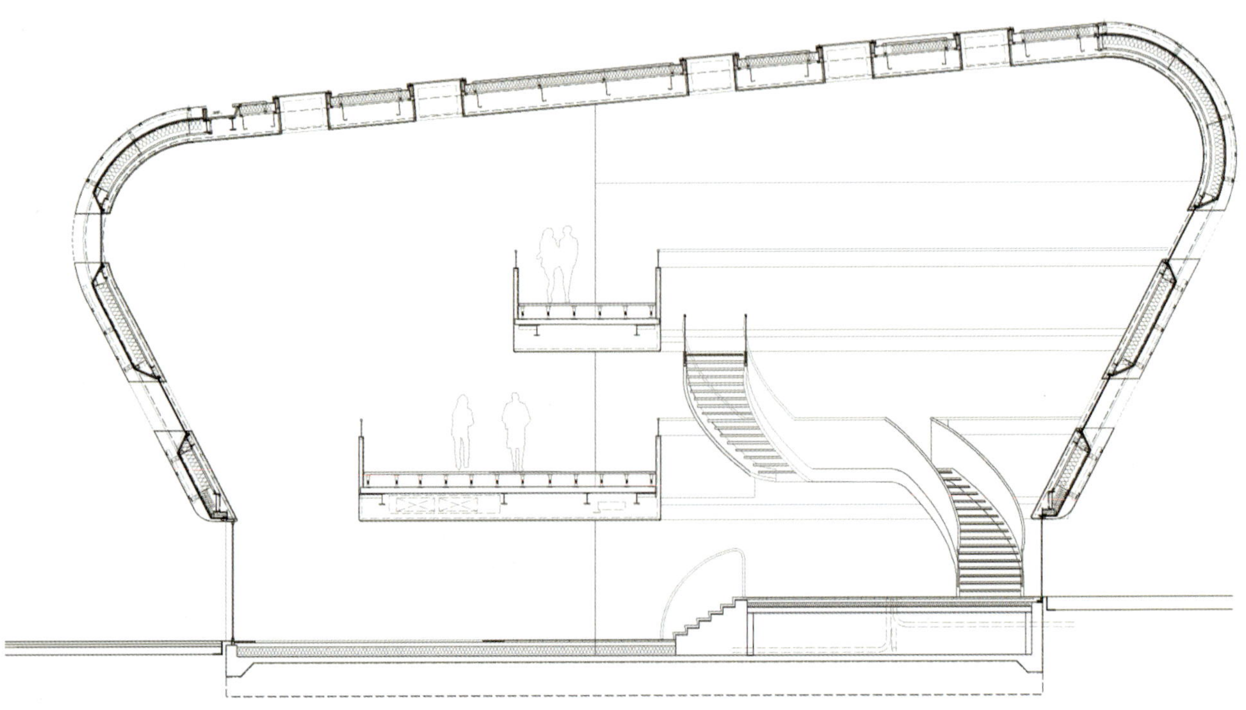

Peter Farmer heads up 3DReid's award-winning Airport and Infrastructure Groups. He is highly active in generating research within the sector, and speaks regularly at major industry conferences. Peter has been working on airports for over 20 years, and during this period he has been involved in every aspect of an airfield's operation. He now has a key understanding of the various pressures and motivations that drive airports the world over.

3DReid
West End House,
11 Hills Place,
London, W1F 7SE
T: 0207 297 5761
www.3dreid.com

The result, a stunning modern design that effortlessly references the form and materials of an aircraft in its sleek, bold lines, is both practical and functional, but it is its striking visual form that has seen it included in a number of films and advertisements, including Inception and James Bond Quantum of Solace.

A commercial project, this private aviation facility had to include a terminal, hangars, an air traffic control tower, and offices for staff and administrators. The design is simple, modern and unselfconscious, using minimal materials and instead relying on the confident use of shape and form to communicate the space. Aviation references are frequent throughout the building, with elements of an airplane such as the fuselage and aerofoil offering a visual presence in the design.

The materiality of the building further communicates the influence of aeronautical engineering on the building. The zinc shingle cladding is key to the aesthetic, providing a reptilian quality to the curvaceous terminal building and Air Traffic Control tower. The effect is lustrous, sleek and sexy, appealing to the successful patrons of the airport whether they be highflying businessmen or celebrities.

The main terminal reception is arresting, and one can't help but stop and take in the space. A white interior with a swirling staircase and balconies cleverly bisects the building, creating a clear distinction between customer spaces and the offices for the airport operator, TAG aviation.

The area surrounding the airport is low lying, and thus it was important to reduce the visual impact of the hangars, the largest element of the facility. Structural engineers Buro Happold were engaged to this end, devising a tiered arch system located below ground. This allows for a column free internal space, creating more room for operational use and lower floor to ceiling heights. The three hangar bays form a single undulating wave, mirroring the topology of the area and further lessening the visual intrusion of the design.

Designed with luxury in mind, this elegant, lavish airport offers the best in structure, engineering and design, ensuring hassle free travel to and from a unique and extravagant terminal.

Photography: Hufton & Crow

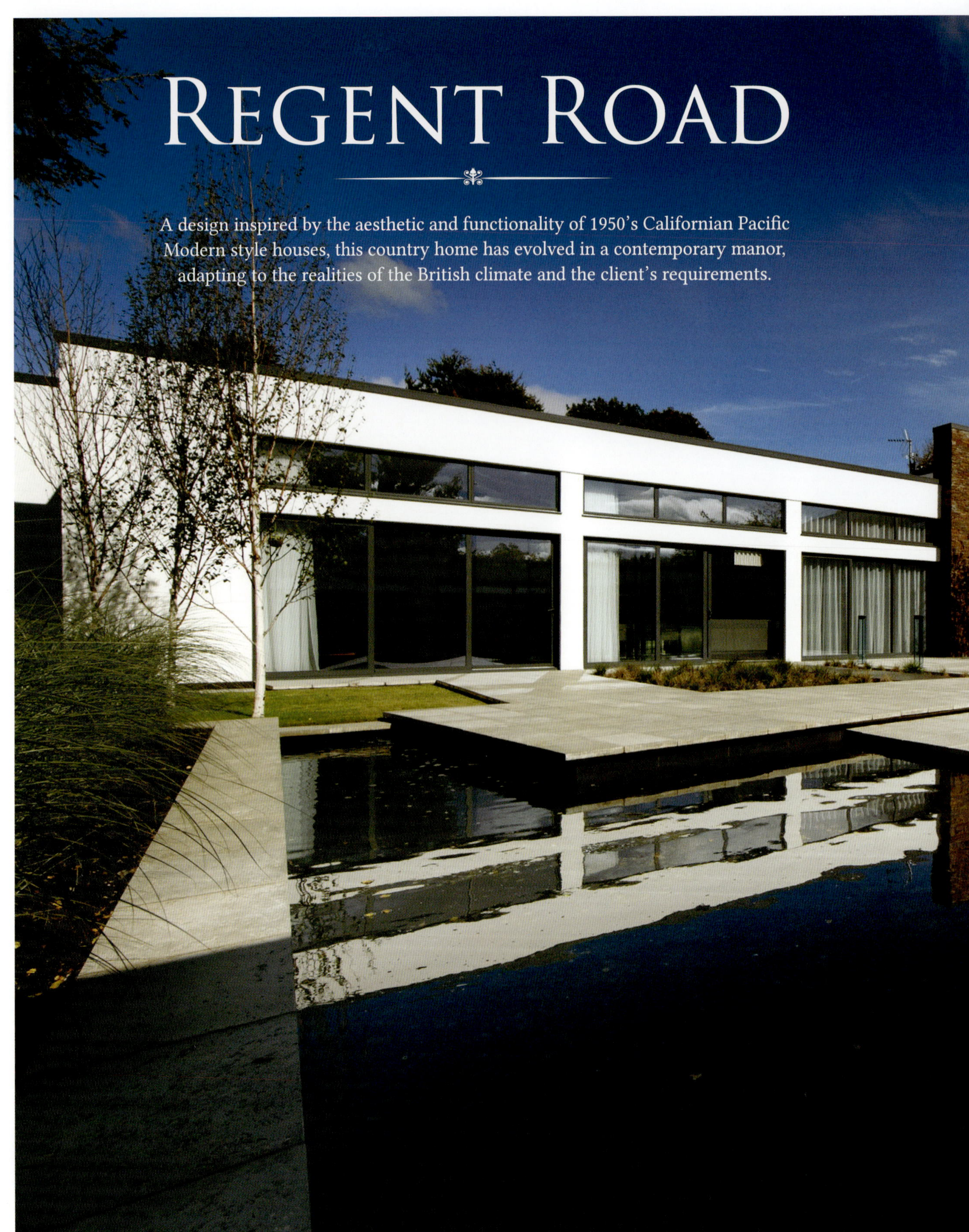

REGENT ROAD

A design inspired by the aesthetic and functionality of 1950's Californian Pacific
Modern style houses, this country home has evolved in a contemporary manor,
adapting to the realities of the British climate and the client's requirements.

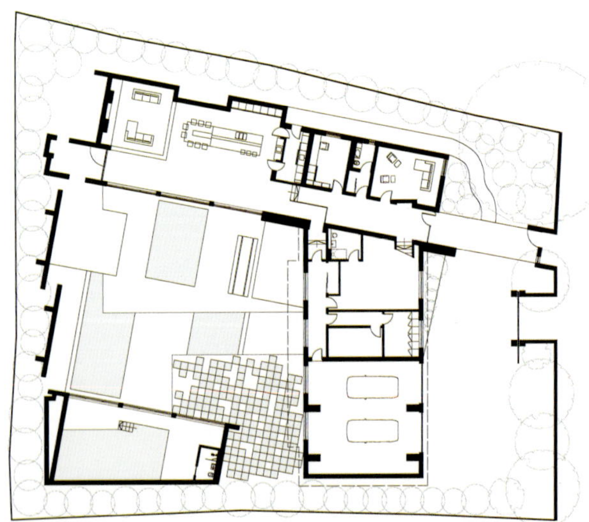

Ground Floor

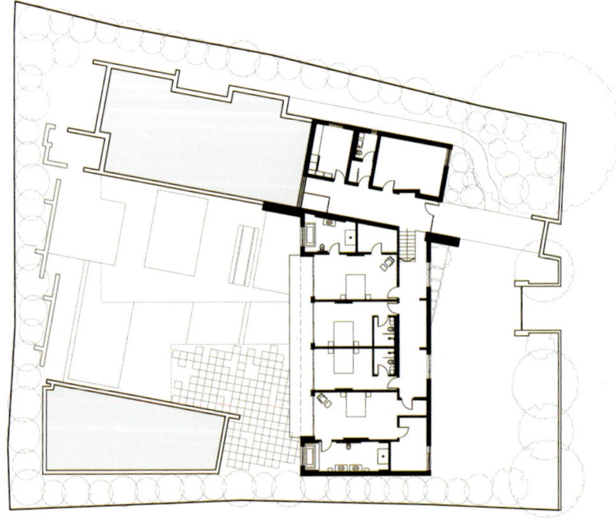

First Floor

Mark Percival, Architecture:m

Architecture:m is a growing, dynamic and creative architectural studio whose philosophy is to delight clients by delivering innovative and comprehensive design solutions. Design, being the cornerstone of the company's philosophy, is achieved by fully understanding the client's needs, being sympathetic to the environment and the guarantee that the most appropriate solution is reached.

Architecture:m Chartered Architects
First Floor,
12 Tariff Street,
Manchester M1 2FF
T: 0161 237 3324
www.architecturem.co.uk

The brief for this contemporary home was both simple and flexible. The clients wanted a home with plenty of communal spaces that would cater for day-to-day family life, joined easily to private spaces for each family member to retreat to.

The shape and orientation of the site saw Architecture:m Chartered Architects implement a home structured to facilitate the kind of living environment that the clients desired. A living wing joins perpendicular to a sleeping, which together create a semi-enclosed courtyard; the courtyard facilitates a secluded feel with well-established trees surrounding the property adding to the tranquil country sensibility.

Contrasting colours and textures with interesting window placement creates a fascinating but refrained façade that acts as a barrier between the public domain and the private arena. With the house turning away from the outside world in this way, the relationship between the internal spaces and the enclosed courtyard is accentuated through generous sized patio doors, balconies and the continuity of materials.

A stone feature wall that runs from the entry through the house acts as a spine from which all other elements emanate. External finishes are purposefully restricted to crisp white render and the graphite grey of the window frames. The angular and textured landscaping to the hidden courtyard is the primary feature of the exterior space. The fractured elements of this landscape design take direct reference from the rhythm and proportion of the house and therefore compliment the building.

White walls continue inside and contrast the stone feature wall and the large format light grey floor tiles. Such a simple palette allows the furniture and artwork to pop. The mirroring of the inside and outside materials perpetuates the easy relationship between in and out.

Enclosing the courtyard formed by the two primary wings of the residence, is an indoor pool and gymnasium. A wall of sliding doors opens this luxurious space to the yard, for a seamless connection with the landscape, which successfully addresses the client's desire for interlinked space.

All construction products were specified with sustainability in mind, encompassing expected lifetime of the product, excellent thermal capacity and limited transportation distance.

Photography: Andrew Haslam

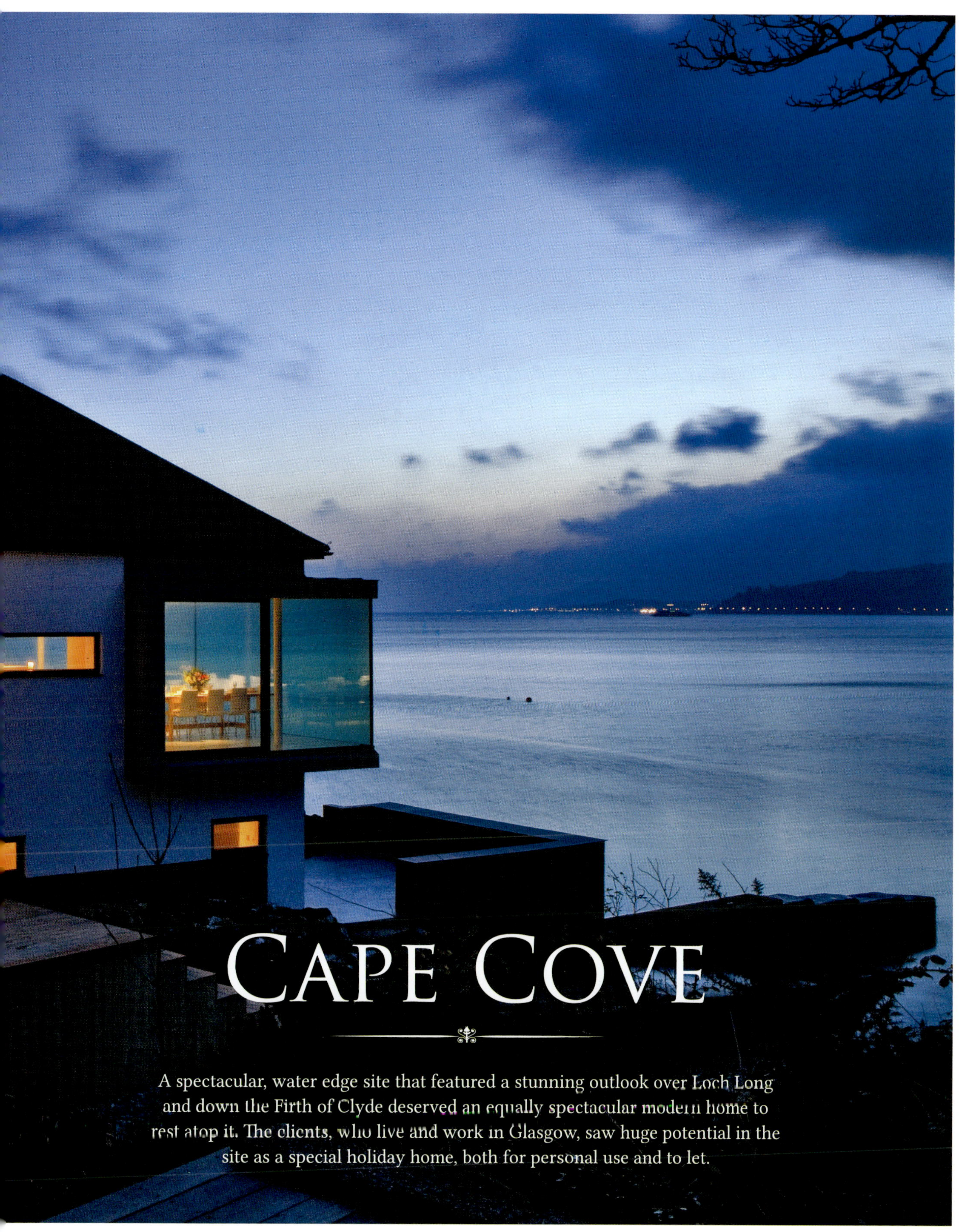

CAPE COVE

A spectacular, water edge site that featured a stunning outlook over Loch Long
and down the Firth of Clyde deserved an equally spectacular modern home to
rest atop it. The clients, who live and work in Glasgow, saw huge potential in the
site as a special holiday home, both for personal use and to let.

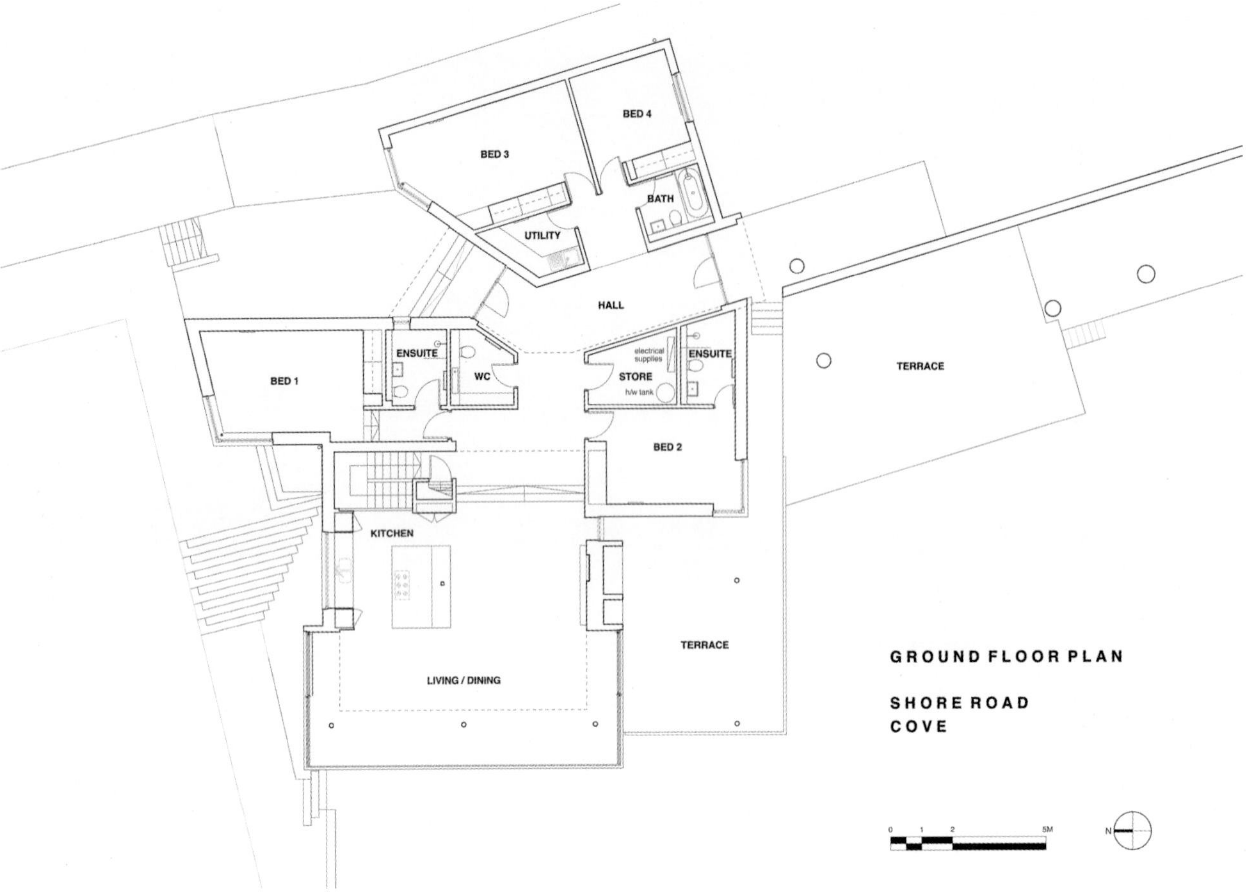
BED 4
BED 3
BATH
UTILITY
HALL
ENSUITE
WC
electrical supplies
STORE
h/w tank
ENSUITE
BED 1
BED 2
TERRACE
KITCHEN
TERRACE
LIVING / DINING
GROUND FLOOR PLAN
SHORE ROAD
COVE
0 1 2 5M
N

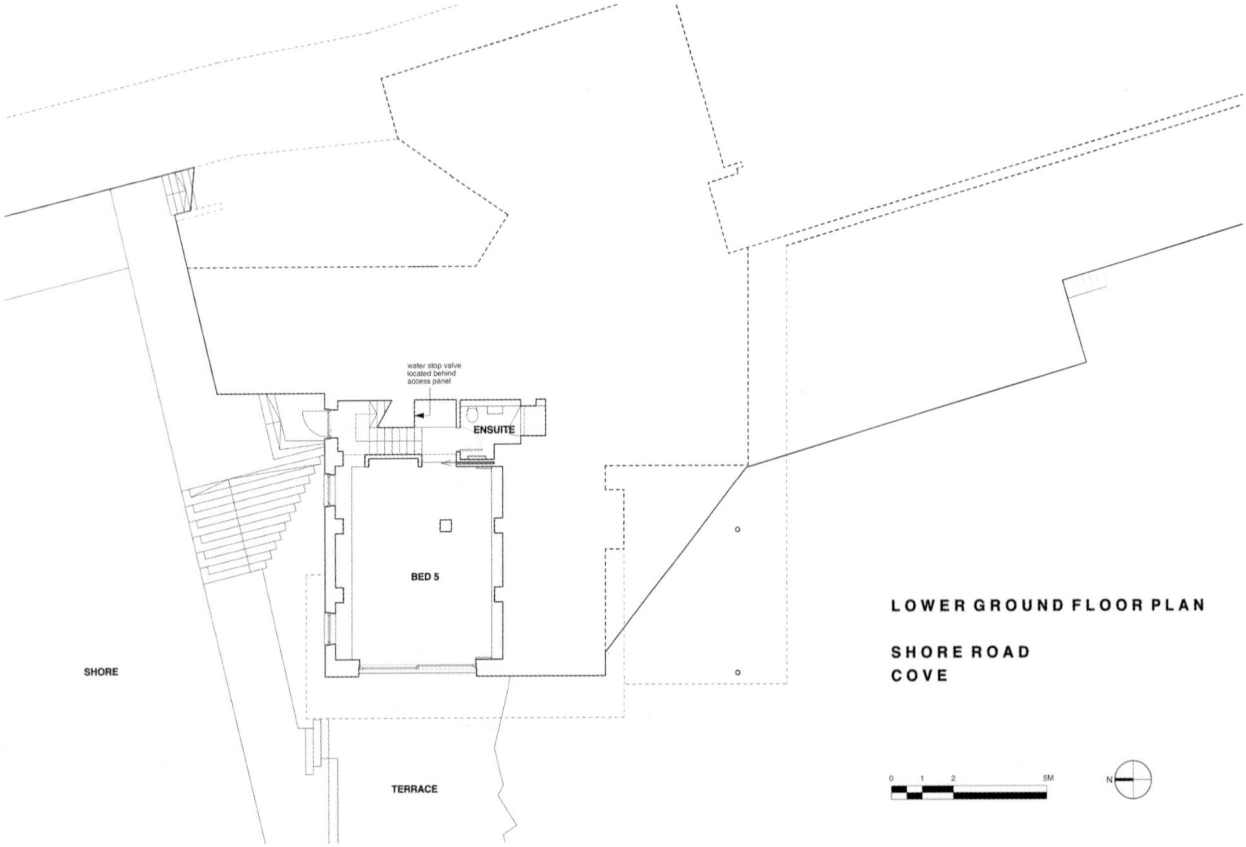
water stop valve located behind access panel
ENSUITE
BED 5
SHORE
TERRACE
LOWER GROUND FLOOR PLAN
SHORE ROAD
COVE
0 1 2 5M
N

A disused naval lookout post built during the Second World War had been converted into a small and uninspiring house on the site some time previously, but this structure failed to take full advantage of the opportunities the location offered. The owners sought to harness the site's potential as a comfortable holiday location in both summer and winter weather, observing the unique possibility to create a vantage point to watch a storm or the occasional surfacing submarine.

For economical reasons, and to pay respect to the history of the site, the existing roof was retained in the new design. The spatial organisation of the house, however, was entirely re-imagined, giving the home a logical flow, which leads to the stunning view over the water and Clyde Estuary. As a result, the entrance hallway is now a large, sunny space that welcomes visitors into the home.

Reconfiguring the approach and entrance to the home had a profound effect on the aspect of the space. The circulation to the principal living areas was adjusted to allow for the division of private spaces, strengthening the big view from the main living zone.

The original kitchen and dining areas were transferred from the ground level to the first floor and extended. Full height frameless glazing has created a dynamic and ever-changing wallpaper for the new spacious and open living, dining and kitchen space. The interior is restrained and simple, with a mixed palette of materials and colours ensuring it neither fades into the background nor demands too much attention. Similarly, the tactile oak surfaces bring a visual warmth to the kitchen and stair core. For comfort, the limestone tiled floor is heated from beneath.

An external teak deck provides access to the private pebble beach adjacent and offers space for a partially covered barbecue deck and hot tub, the latter of which is positioned to enjoy the unique and uninterrupted view down the loch.

Cameronwebster Architects
The Printworks,
10 Otago Street,
Glasgow G12 8JH
T: 0141 330 9898
www.cameronwebster.com

Photography: Darple Photography

HOXTON

A complicated arrangement of pokey rooms stacked over several stories comprised
the Hoxton House, a typical 19th Century terrace home in England.

living
void
Ground
kitchen
dining
rear
garden
Basement

Working closely with clients to make exceptional custom-designed homes, each project produced by David Mikhail Architects is unique, tailored to brief and location.

Established in 1992 and based in Clerkenwell Green, London, their work has achieved numerous awards and has been widely published both in the United Kingdom and abroad. The projects represent excellent value for their clients and are often created within tight budgetary constraints.

David Mikhail Architects
10-11 Clerkenwell Green,
London EC1R 0DP
T: 0207 608 1505
www.davidmikhail.com

The kitchen was located underground in a semi-basement under a ceiling height of only two metres. A small rear courtyard was part of the home's saving grace, affording the owners some much desired outdoor space on their tight urban lot. Access to this space, however, was via a half landing off a cramped service staircase down to the kitchen.

Desiring a new kitchen and dining area that permitted relaxation and conversation whilst food was being prepared, as well as an elegant space to entertain friends and family, the young couple who own the home employed David Mikhail, confident that his ingenuity would provide them with a perfect outcome.

Mikhail successfully transformed this disordered home into one that suited the couple's modern condition, and did so in a way that was modest in scale but grand in architectural order.

The new rooms have essentially been carved from the original terrace house, permitting the rear courtyard to remain and the rooms to engage actively with it. An extension of only one metre allows for the new above-ground kitchen, dining area, sitting area and bathroom. By slotting the new spaces more or less within the envelope of the existing property, the potential for engagement with the courtyard has been unlocked.

The bespoke double-story cruciform façade has been engineered from high quality Douglas fir and structurally bonded double-glazing. The double height does much to challenge the home's original aesthetic whilst at the same time lightly and effortlessly blending with it.

A bright white kitchen reflects the light brought in through extensive glazing as does the white concrete floor, offset by natural materials and the warm brick hues of the small courtyard. A void extends over the dining area, affording the space a sense of openness once thought impossible in such a small property. Above the kitchen, a sitting room – contained inside a practically invisible glass balustrade – is a lovely space to recline and relax overlooking the rear courtyard.

Chic and stylish, these interior spaces are decorated with pieces that make a modern reference to eras past while at the same time celebrating the contemporary nature of its makeover. Warm tones of green and orange articulate a stand-out décor, perfectly complementing what is a unique and impressive remodel.

Photography: Tim Crocker

TERRACE

This refurbishment and extension to an early 20th Century house on a narrow block provides the residents with more space and new rooms in a contemporary, modular re-imagination of the original property.

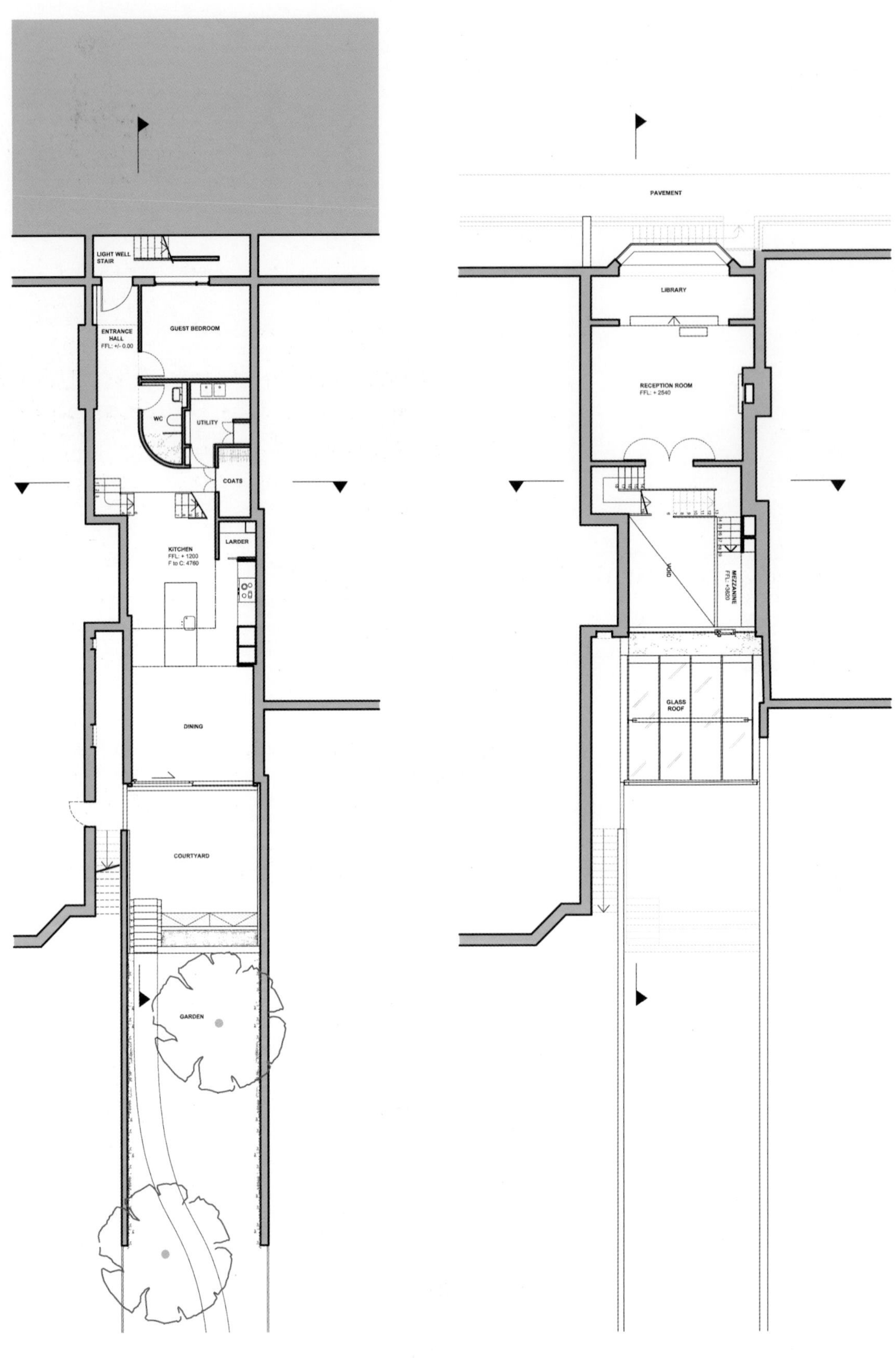

BASEMENT / EXTENSION LEVEL PLAN

UPPER GROUND FLOOR PLAN

David Mikhail Architects
10-11 Clerkenwell Green,
London EC1R 0DP
T: 0207 608 1505
www.davidmikhail.com

This small extension, slipped between two larger terrace properties, used to be a library adjoining the house. This reconfiguration represents an architectural triumph for the designers, highlighting the advantages of the site and turning an unattractive and no longer functional space into an aspect of the home that adds value and ultimately exceeds the customer's expectations of what could be achieved.

The refurbishment included the construction of a double garage and photography studio in matte black, adding two new functional spaces to the property. The home and the studio/garage bookend the narrow property, creating a haven-like garden between these contrasting buildings.

The interior is pervaded by a sense of ingenuity, with custom spaces either discreet or featured depending on their use. The laundry room is unobtrusive and tastefully hidden, but the gallery and study area overlooks the kitchen and garden room, creating a dialogue between the two spaces and uniting them in a central feature of the house.

The glazed garden room – far from being an afterthought – is a re-evaluation of interior verses exterior space, drawing the garden into the kitchen and through the open house, allowing a flood of light into all the spaces.

A sophisticated palette enhances the bright, fresh feeling of the house. Light grey and white, broken only by coffee coloured timber floors afford this home a sense of unparalleled modernity and elegance.

Photography: Tim Crocker

Raasay Community Hall

Handsome and humble, this expansive timber-clad building on the Scottish island of Raasay serves as a local community hall and has become a central hub of social activity. Designed as a multipurpose building to serve an almost innumerable list of requirements, the elegant functionality of the space is undeniable. In addition, the warmth of the design is such that it stops the hall from becoming simply an industrial and utilitarian fixture.

Mary Arnold-Forster is a principal with Dualchas Building Design, based in Skye and Glasgow. Having been with the practice for 12 years, she has been responsible for some 40 houses in that time. Mary was the architect behind the Raasay Community Hall, which recently won a RIBA award, as well as the new hall currently under construction on Muck.

Mary specialises in sustainable architecture in peripheral locations, and is committed to using renewable technologies. She has both worked and written for The Lighthouse, taught at Aberdeen, Dundee, The London Metropolitan and The Prince of Wales university, and has lectured in England, Scotland and Wales.

The local community sought a robust building - one that would meet their diverse and occasionally competing needs on a tight budget. Not only that, but they hoped for something that would sit comfortably on a site that could easily be compromised by an unattractive building. The resulting simple design is an ideal solution. Used frequently by the school, the hairdresser, local musicians, the church and art classes just to name a few, it is a perfect venue for concerts and sporting events. Timeless and enduring, this quietly stated hall has, in many ways, exceeded its brief.

The building makes a bold statement when approached. The façade is clad entirely in local larch, which extends from the walls over the roof. The design itself is based on the shape and form of a simple agricultural shed, but the materiality and attention to detail give the building a contemporary edge and ensure it rests comfortably on the site.

The site's appreciable 30% slope presented a challenge for the designers. To overcome this obstacle, entrances suitable for disabled access into the building were added at both upper and lower levels, thus avoiding an expensive and heavy maintenance lift. Further improving the economy of the hall, the structure is heated using a ground-source heat pump and heat recovery system, which keep thermal costs at a minimum.

Inside, the building houses a multi-purpose hall, meeting room, storage spaces, offices, showering and water closet facilities. Oak floors and birch faced ply walls enhance the feeling of natural warmth and the uncomplicated, functional aesthetic that the hall embodies. Built for badminton, the birch lined hall's extensive glazing makes it a visual focal point both inside and outside the building. Adding to the practical aspect of the space, a large catering kitchen featuring stainless steel appliances is also included.

Dualchas Building Design
Duisdale Beag,
Sleat, Isle of Skye IV43 8QU
T: 0147 183 3300
www.dualchas.com

Photography: Andrew Lee

TOWER HOUSE

Powerful, modern and sophisticated with a hint of raw texture, the Tower House
by Edgley Design rises from the dense foliage of the Caribbean island hillside
upon which it sits, rendered in pale green to blend into the tropical palette.

Edgley Design is a United Kingdom-based Royal Institute of British Architects Chartered architectural practice with a wide range of experience from residential new build and refurbishment to property development and urban master planning.

They love to build, and their passion is creating spaces, places and objects that are a pleasure to live with, work with and admire, whatever the constraints of context and brief.

Edgley believe that architecture in the 21st century demands a sustainable approach to problem solving and that design needs to return to natural processes and materials, which in turn will promote a return to buildings that are tuned to their environment and context.

Edgley Design
Studio 2.07,
12-18 Hoxton Street,
London N1 6NG
T: 0207 033 9522
www.edgleydesign.co.uk

Inspired by traditional Moroccan courtyard houses, this five-bedroom residence on a steep hillside on the dense jungle island of Bequia provides a series of intimate spaces surrounding a central pool that is sheltered from the sun and gently cools the home as warm breezes blow across the water.

This modern home is a reinterpretation of what has become traditional in contemporary design, embracing the hot climate by incorporating large open spaces and overhanging roofs. Spaces are vertical rather than horizontal, accentuating the steep section of the house and providing a dramatic spatial experience. The building is laid out along three axis, with the courtyard looking out over the pool to the hills beyond, and two wings looking out to the bays either side.

The house offers a series of experiences revealed as you move toward and through it. The site is accessed along a winding mountain road from above, and as you descend the steep drive all that can be seen is the long, low wall that serves as the back of the main hall. A single window gives a view through the house to the sea, but the overall impression is of a modest, private house.

A delicate balcony entrance is suspended high over a steep drop, and from this platform visitors to the site are afforded the first glimpse of the dramatic views down the hillside to the bay beyond.

This leads to the mezzanine level, and the spaces of the house open out to the courtyard surrounding the pool. The bedroom towers frame the view of the distant islands.

Sequential home design allows the house to step down the steep hillside, generating a natural shift from public to private with spaces that unfold as you move deeper into the house.

Photography: Jake Edgley

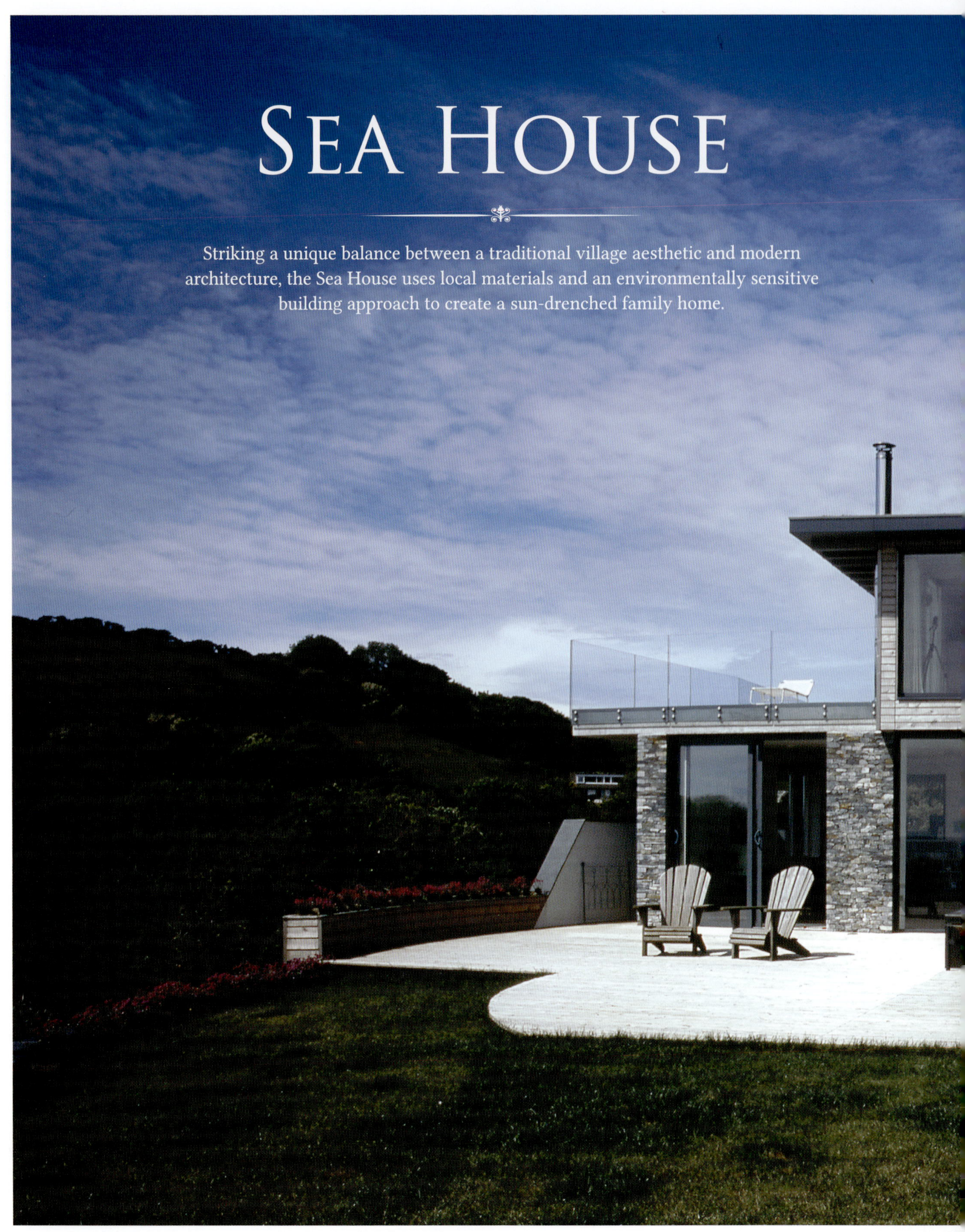

SEA HOUSE

Striking a unique balance between a traditional village aesthetic and modern architecture, the Sea House uses local materials and an environmentally sensitive building approach to create a sun-drenched family home.

First Floor

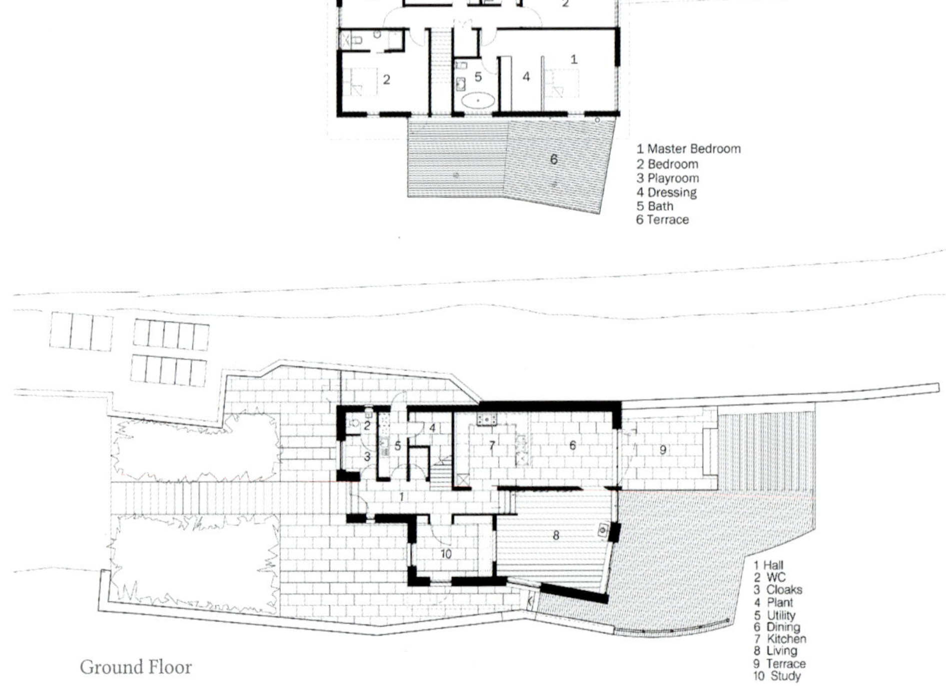

Ground Floor

After working in Italy and gaining experience in the offices of Peter Aldington, Will Alsop and Norman Foster, Robert Evans set up Evans Vettori with Mariangela Vettori in 1995. They opened their Matlock studio in the picturesque Derbyshire Dales, and have since built up a highly acclaimed, design-led practice dedicated to sensitive and sustainable modern architecture.

Evans Vettori has developed a specialism in education work, particularly for people with special needs, and have an increasingly high profile both in their locality and nationally. They have won many design awards and have work regularly published in books and the architectural press.

Evans Vettori
31 Knowleston Pl Matlock, GB
T: +44 (0) 01 629 760 559
www.evansvettori.co.uk

This modern yet cosy beachside home on the Roseland Peninsula in South Cornwall, United Kingdom, emphasizes and enhances its location in an area of outstanding natural beauty. Perched above Portloe, a charming fishing village, and located in a conservation area on the heritage coast, the façade was carefully considered and the modern yet unobtrusive design sits naturally against the rise of the hill.

The design comprises two stories, the lower consisting of natural Cornish slate that was laid in semi-dry, giving the exterior a dry stone wall effect that is both natural and relaxed. Atop the slate lower floor is a wooden box containing the bedrooms. This rests against the hillside, allowing for a large timber deck that provides a magnificent panoramic view of Jacka Point and the English Channel beyond.

Views of the ocean are integral to the design. The house acts as a telescope, magnifying the ocean as you approach and enter the house, maximizing the eastward sea views across the channel. Extensive, floor to ceiling glazing throughout the house further augments the views, and the living area is 'kinked' to open the space outward.

The interior is relaxed, comfortable and modern. Downstairs, an open-plan living area gives the family common spaces to eat, work and relax. The study area offers a commanding view of the sea and allows the clients to work comfortably from home in a tranquil, informal environment. Upstairs, a more traditional layout offers four bedrooms, three bathrooms and a playroom, providing private spaces for the family of four.

Balancing the needs of the client against the unique challenges and advantages of the site, the gently stepped profile and the natural, local materials of the design combine on site to make the best of a picturesque location.

Photography: Peter Blundell Jones and Nigel Rigden

BERKSHIRE

This substantial modern country house is set within twelve acres of elevated grounds on the banks of the River Thames in Berkshire.

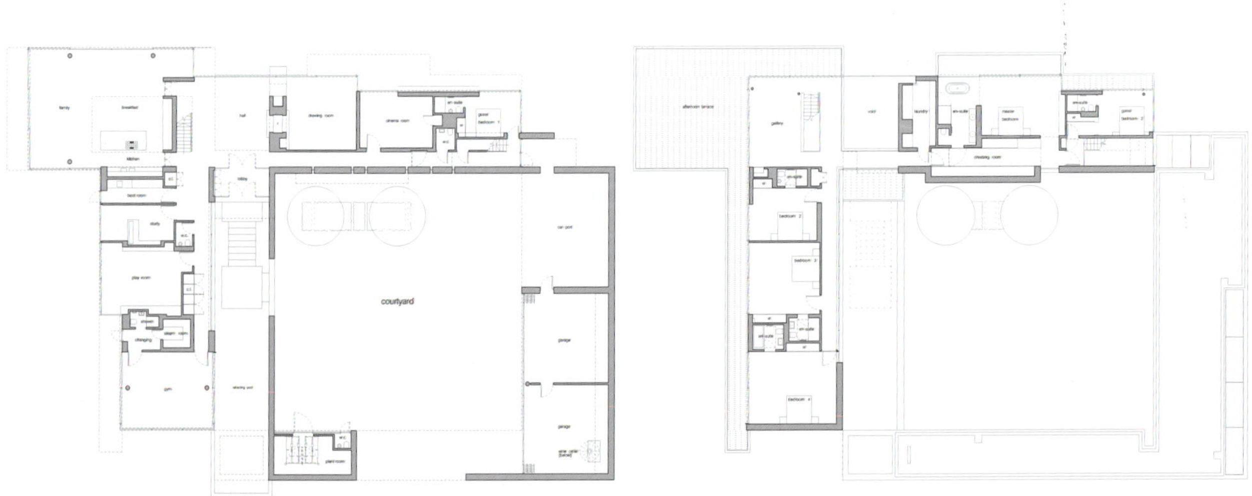

Ground Floor

First Floor

A member of both the British Institute of Interior Design and the Royal Institute of British Architects, Gregory Phillips established his practice in 1991. Gregory Phillips Architects has since earned a widespread reputation for the high calibre of its design work, winning several awards and much recognition. The Practice ethos is one of fully understanding the client's needs, sensitively translating these into designs of the highest standard.

Gregory Phillips Architects
17 Savile Row, London W1S 3PN
T: 020 7724 3040
www.gregoryphillips.com

The layout of the house evolved from a simple diagram incorporating a protected centralised courtyard flanked by glazed single-aspect rooms affording magnificent countryside views, inspired by traditional country houses with adjoining stable yards.

This line drawing evolved into a restrained plan of generously-proportioned spaces surrounding a flint-walled inner-courtyard linked by galleried corridors faced with timber panelling and stone floors.

The extensive contemporary flint-work used within the courtyard reinterprets the flint-work within the surrounding village, and in particular the medieval church that is within view of the property. The horizontal strips of render almost extend and reinforce the contours of the site when viewing the property from the river.

The site is accessed via a pair of grand, Grade I Listed metal gates and a gravelled driveway leading to the central courtyard which is completely enclosed by the house and out-buildings.

Entry to the house itself is made by crossing an enclosed reflecting pool leading into a double height space. From here the building is predominantly glazed to face the far-reaching north-western views with terracing at each level.

The gardens immediately adjacent to the house incorporate an infinity edged swimming pool and a tennis court, the landscaping follows a simple, semi-formal layout which leads on to the extensive grounds and open-countryside beyond.

A concrete structure was built up to and including first floor level with a steel frame above. The house became the first residence within the UK to incorporate a Cobiax slab at first floor level in order to achieve the extensive cantilevers inherent within the design.

The local planning authority requested a dwelling of architectural merit in order to replace the much smaller dwelling previously situated upon the site. This project certainly delivered on that request.

Photography: Darren Chung

GUILDFORD

Built in the mid 1800s, this beautiful Victorian home had been afforded a Grade II Listed status. Set within twenty acres near Guildford, the substantial home had previously been subjected to extensive alteration and expansion, which had compromised the original house, leaving it an unlikely shell for a confusing array of uncomfortably proportioned interior spaces.

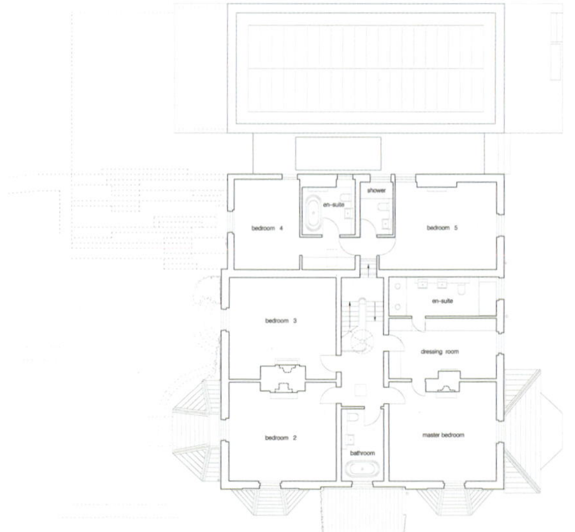

First Floor

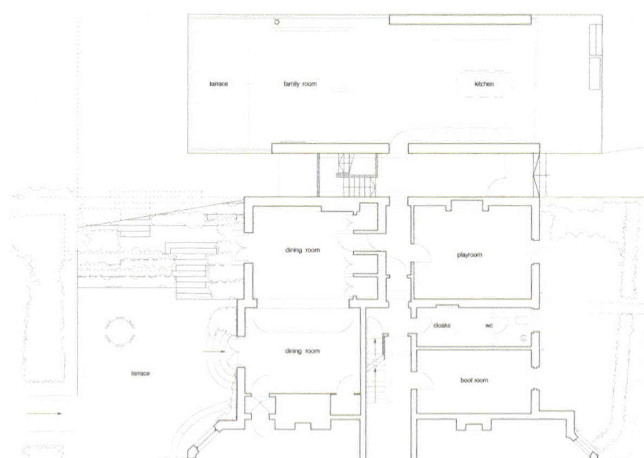

Ground Floor

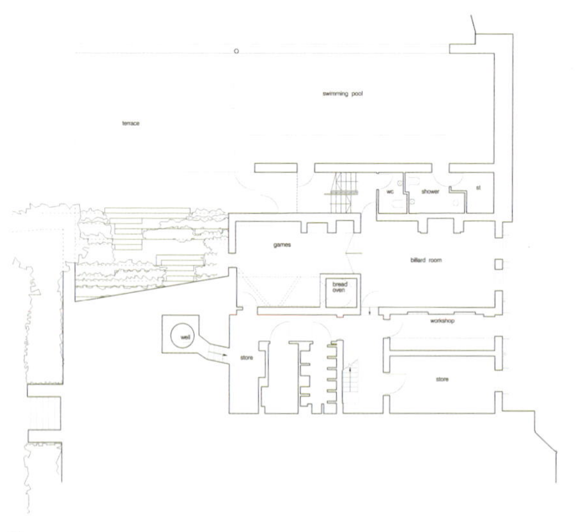

Basement

In tackling this project, the new renovation sought to undo the clumsy alterations to the original home, reinstating the traditional configuration and circulation of the home and restoring the interior of the main house and introducing a contemporary rear extension. The inspiring setting and the beauty of the original home beckoned for a dynamic intervention, which would fully utilise the property.

The main house, incorporating a number of reception rooms, lacked the large spaces suitable for 21st century living. The existing dining room was therefore elegantly extended into the area behind, previously an array of small spaces on different levels.

A two storey addition to the rear of the home has been designed in a modernist architectural language, providing a strong contrast to the traditional form of the house. The addition complements the simple rendered façade of the original Victorian house. The extension relates equally well to the main house and the gentle contours of the surrounding garden.

The external proportions of the new extension have been carefully considered in relation to the mass of the existing property, ensuring its impact on the profile of the home is minimal. The glazed link between the spaces is recessed from the main façade, and its height has been carefully matched to existing horizontal projections, differentiating old and new and ensuring an elegant, understated transition.

Projects at this level of historical importance and magnitude are rarely carried off with such grace and respect for the original structures. This stunning renovation and reimagining of the property on this site reworks a convoluted interior and clarifies the existing property, updating it for modern living.

Photography: Darren Chung

Gregory Phillips Architects
17 Savile Row, London W1S 3PN
T: 020 7724 3040
www.gregoryphillips.com

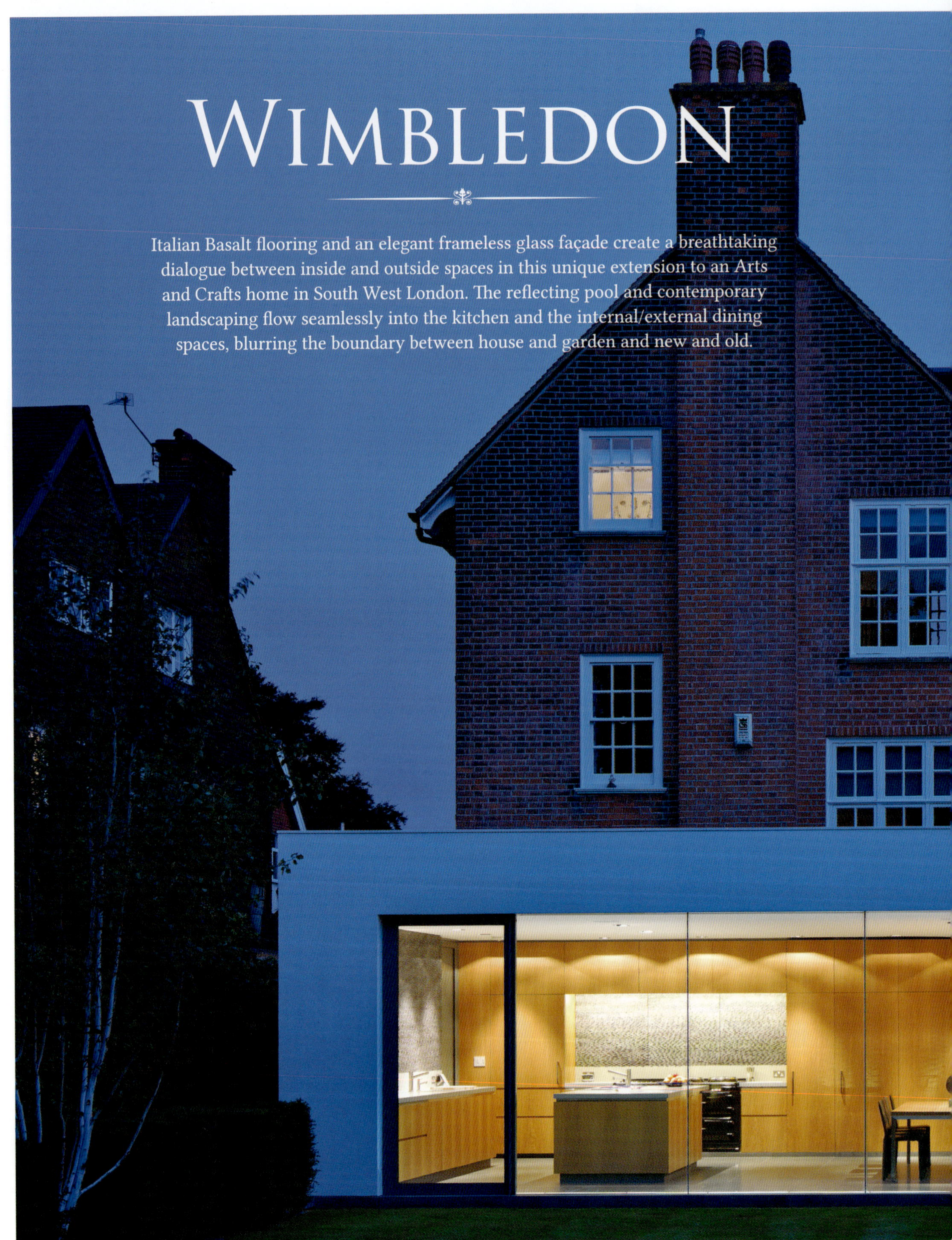

WIMBLEDON

Italian Basalt flooring and an elegant frameless glass façade create a breathtaking
dialogue between inside and outside spaces in this unique extension to an Arts
and Crafts home in South West London. The reflecting pool and contemporary
landscaping flow seamlessly into the kitchen and the internal/external dining
spaces, blurring the boundary between house and garden and new and old.

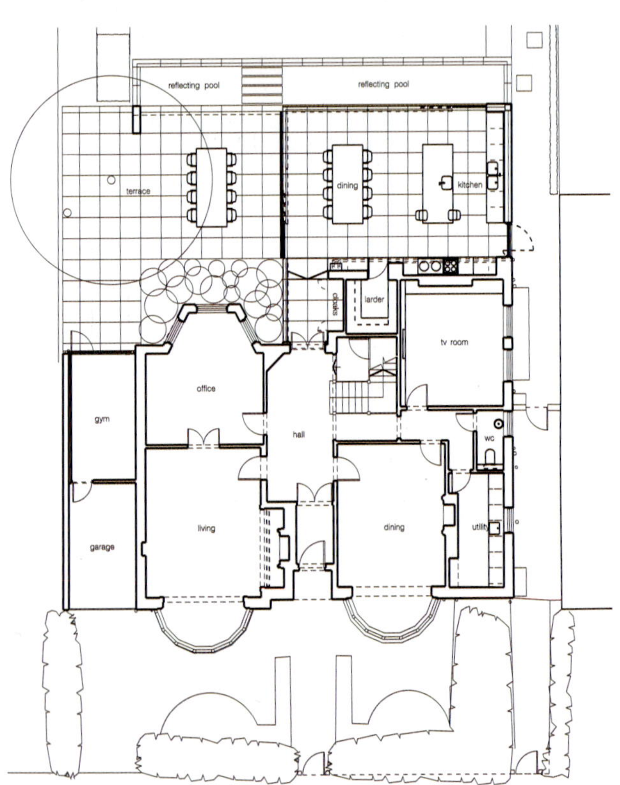

Ground Floor

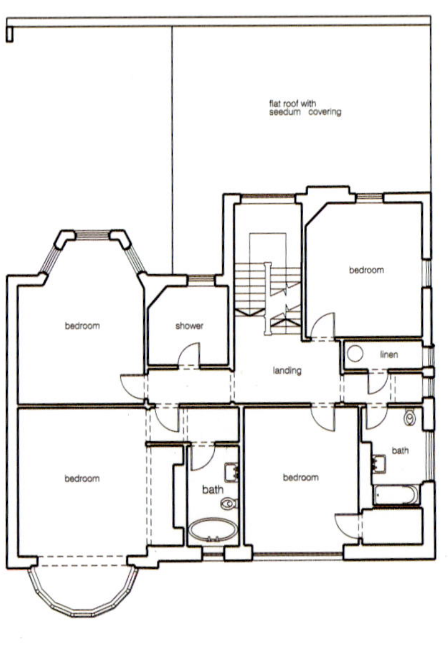

First Floor

This exceptional kitchen addition is small, but the custom oak cabinetry and the sleek use of stone and glass brings grandeur to the design that gives it substance against the beautiful historical home it adjoins. The unambiguous, highly modern form of the addition is achieved with straight, clean lines and a blend of natural materials.

Italian Basalt flooring both inside and outside tie the al fresco dining area and the new kitchen together, a strong connection that is maintained by a bold white box that extends to frame both spaces. The frameless glass creates a minimal visual barrier between the spaces, which gently mirror one another.

The bespoke cabinetry is sophisticated and refined. The oak veneer is inviting and bright, balancing the neutral Italian Basalt floor. Above the worktop and recessed aga area, a chiseled stone wall forms a minimal yet striking contemporary feature.

The reflecting pool forms a subtle moat around the new space and adds to the sense of grandeur, providing a transitional element between the highly architectural addition and the stylish contemporary landscaped garden.

Functional elements of the design do not compete with the aesthetic strength of the addition. Under-floor heating and concealed air-conditioning provide an elegant solution to artificial climate control. Electric blinds hidden in a slot above the frameless window ensure that light conditions can be easily controlled.

Fantastic modern craftsmanship and the balanced, restrained form of the addition ensure that the beautiful new kitchen doesn't compete with the historic home, but instead forms a modern complement in a contemporary architectural language.

Gregory Phillips Architects
17 Savile Row, London W1S 3PN
T: 020 7724 3040
www.gregoryphillips.com

Photography: Darren Chung

STRANGE HOUSE

Warmth and unobtrusive logic inform the design of this family home.

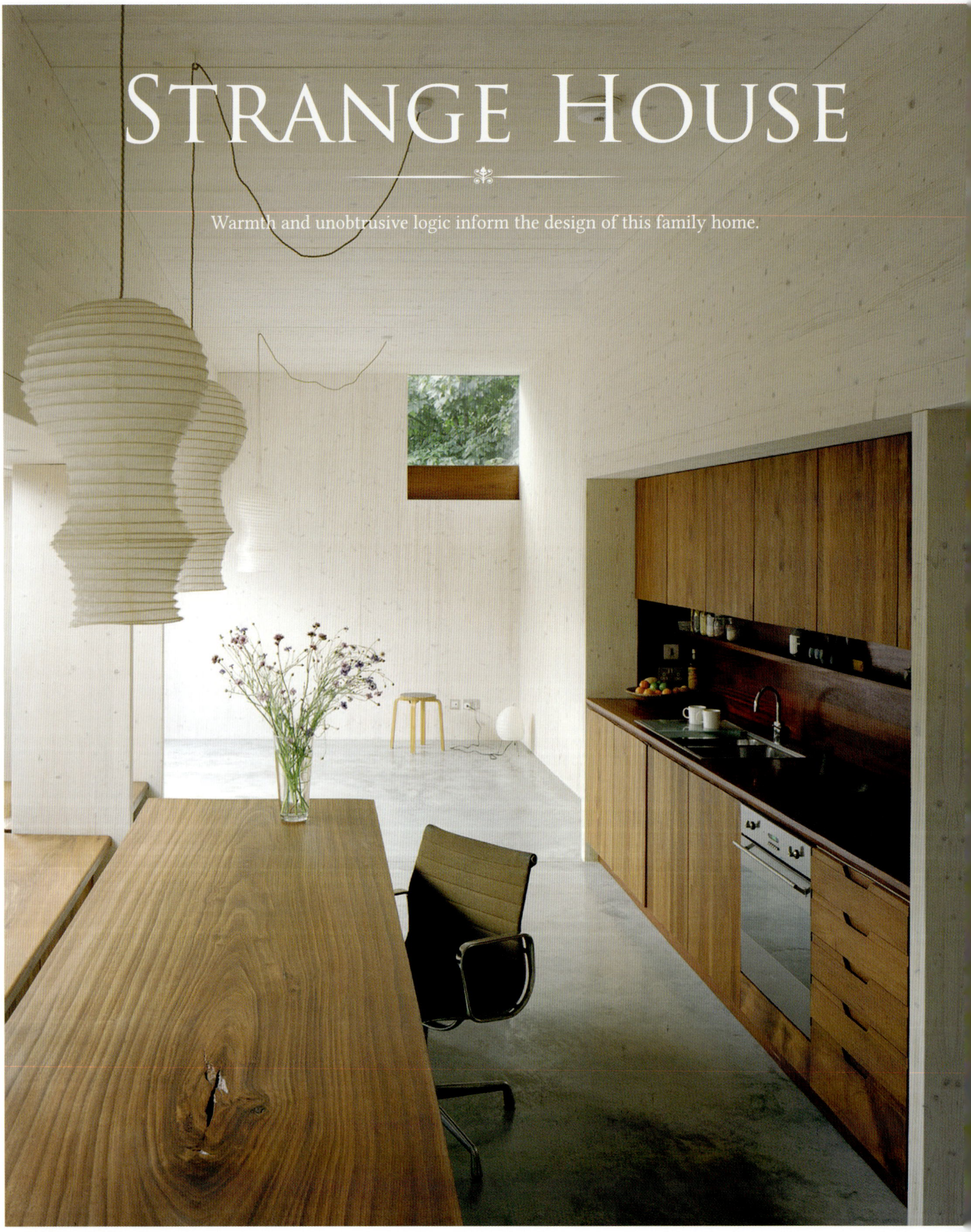

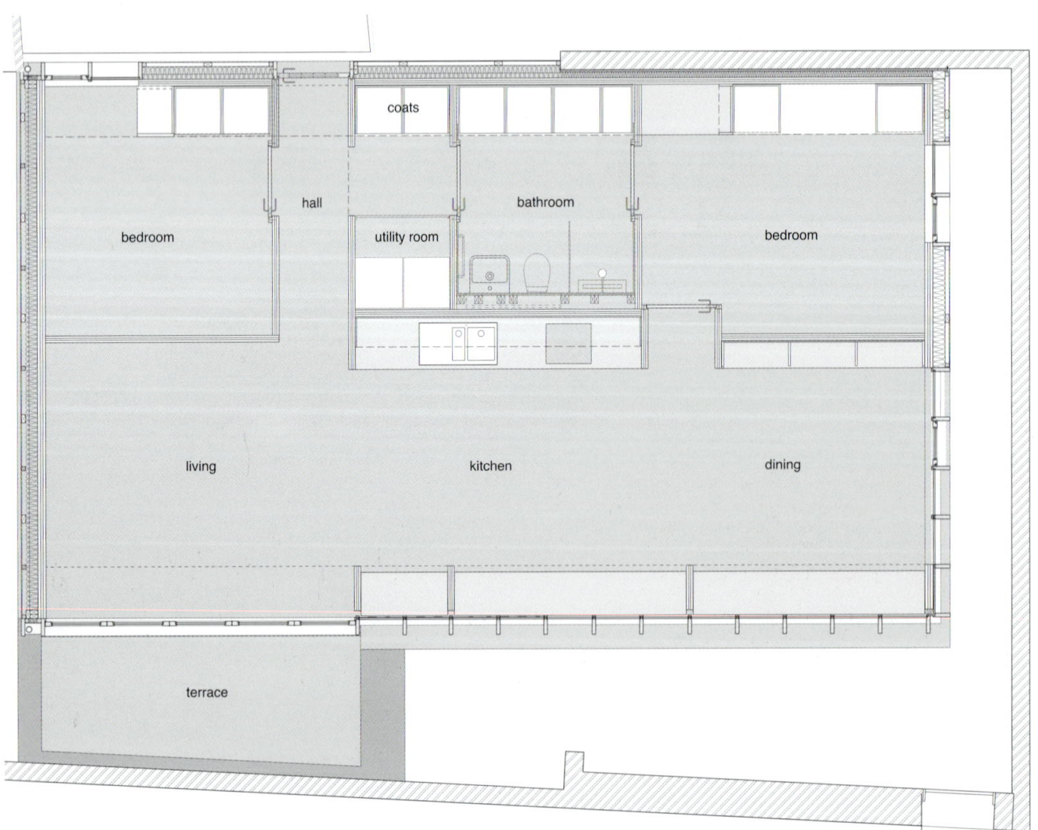

coats
hall
bathroom
bedroom
utility room
bedroom
living
kitchen
dining
terrace

Established in 2010 following the construction of the Strange House – architect Hugh Strange's family home – Hugh Strange Architects is a practice concerned with architecture as a constructive art. Hugh Strange architects are an intelligent practice, forming specific approaches to environmental and structural situations and challenges.

Hugh Strange studied at Edinburgh University and worked for a number of design-led practices in London.

Hugh Strange Architects
210 Evelyn Street,
London SE8 5BZ
T: 0774 070 3940
www.hughstrange.com

Combining the desire for a low budget house on a constrained site that was environmentally sound and spacious enough for a growing family was a challenge, well met with a design that adheres rigorously to a sensible acknowledgment of the union of materials. The feel of a family home however, comes from the attention to detail, the textural juxtapositions and the careful consideration of the house's geometry that Strange and his team attended to.

Located in London's southeast, it is located rather inauspiciously in what was once a pub garden. The block is mostly concealed from the nearby street by an existing perimeter wall. From the street the house looks like nothing so much as a warehouse. It is unassuming, a narrow door in the brickwork giving only a glimpse of the elegant family home behind the wall.

Rather than setting the home immediately against the stone perimeter, slim gaps form a narrow path around the property. These slender walkways allow the home to breathe in the small space it is afforded, and enhance the sense of cosiness the space embodies. The old brickwork speaks to the history of the site, and this links a thematic concern of the house – the juxtaposition of materials to create a striking, emotional space.

The foundations of the house comprise two concrete slabs. The old slab is visible around the garden, and the new slab forms a small terrace, extending into the home as a polished concrete floor.

This abundance of concrete could seem cold, but timber furniture, internal cladding and detail afford the interior space an undeniable warmth. The kitchen, cupboard, seating and shelving units in the entry living space sit within recesses formed in the frame, acknowledging the logic and order the house embodies.

Though it is so small – the house itself only 75m2 – high ceilings throughout the property and long rooms make the house feel palatial. With the large sliding door open, the internal house borrows the existing external brick walls, extending the internal space outwards and making the house feel even larger. The modest courtyard however, reigns this open feeling in, blocking out the city beyond and creating a private world for the family.

Photography: David Grandorge

QUEEN SQUARE

Originally constructed as a family home in the late 1700s, centuries of repairs,
additions and renovations left this Grade II listed property in central London
with a deteriorating façade and a fundamentally confused interior.

Patrick Inglis

Jamal Badrashi

Kim Loddo

Inglis Badrashi Loddo has been recognised as one of the country's most promising young practices as a part of the Architecture Foundation's Next Generation Architects. Principal designers Patrick Inglis, Jamal Badrashi and Kim Loddo, all graduates of Cambridge University, set up the practice in London in 2001 and have completed projects in locations ranging from the Yorkshire Dales to Barcelona.

**Inglis Badrashi Loddo
11 Wells Mews,
London, W1T 3HD
T: 0207 580 8808
www.ibla.co.uk**

Tasked with the re-conversion of this property from ancillary accommodation for an office building back to a family dwelling, Inglis Badrashi Loddo have reinstated this glorious Georgian to its former grandeur with a daring modern twist.

The new design is a careful synthesis of both traditional and modern forms. The existing façade has been carefully restored, refreshing the street presence of the structure. A new structurally glazed extension to the top of the house provides access to the new roof terrace, and gives only a hint, at street level, of the charming contemporary update the house has undergone within.

A dialogue between the restored existing features like the windows and shutters and the new contemporary elements like the staircase and paneling was established as a way to ensure that the new modern elements of the house would relate to the existing historic fabric of the structure. To this end, tonal and textural palettes have been carefully integrated throughout the home. In the entrance hallway a traditional black and white tiled floor made of dust-pressed tiles was laid, recalling a traditional flooring option. This provides a strong juxtaposition against the strikingly modern staircase and the bold form of the curved walnut paneling.

The design of the staircase became the key to the experience of the house, as it linked the large number of floors in the high, rather than wide, property. On the lower floors, the stair was designed to occupy a long narrow slot, maximizing the sense of space for the kitchen and living room and linking them together. Throughout the bedroom floors, the stair transforms into a more traditional running stair, culminating in the glazed box that provides access to the terrace and the wonderful views over the rooftops of Bloomsbury.

The thermal fabric of the home was upgraded to contemporary standards, and new electrically operated vents at the top of the glazed extension were incorporated to set up a stack effect, allowing natural ventilation of the main rooms via the staircase.

In refusing to take the path of least resistance, recreating the Georgian house that once stood here, this design successfully preserves the charming façade of an historically significant home and integrates a functional, beautiful and importantly, sympathetic modern interior. Elements of understated luxury are a base note to the subtle blend of traditional and contemporary design elements that draw this beautiful home together.

Photography: David Grandorge

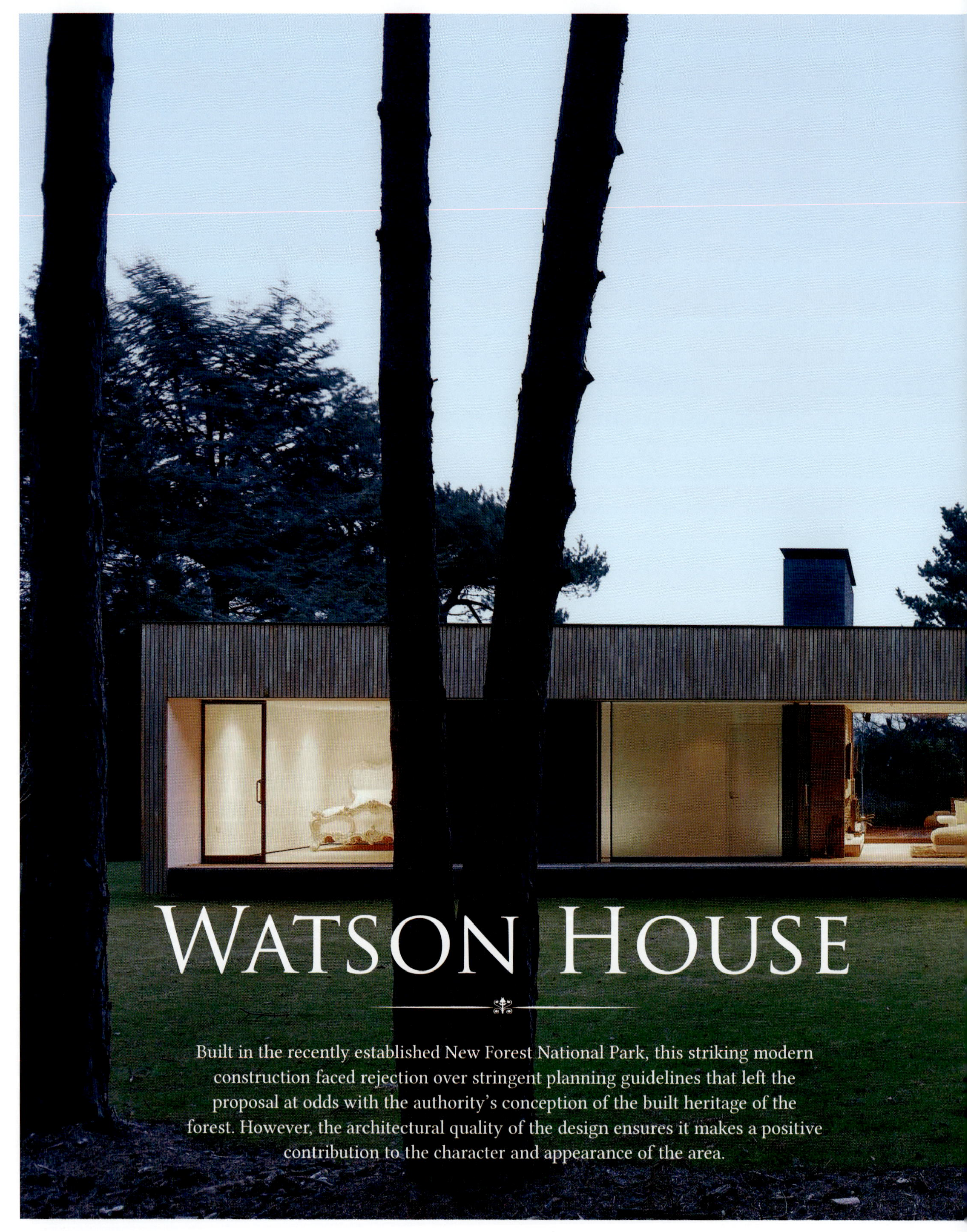

WATSON HOUSE

Built in the recently established New Forest National Park, this striking modern construction faced rejection over stringent planning guidelines that left the proposal at odds with the authority's conception of the built heritage of the forest. However, the architectural quality of the design ensures it makes a positive contribution to the character and appearance of the area.

John Pardey studied architecture at the South Bank Polytechnic, finishing his degree in 1981 and earning his Diploma with Distinction at the Polytechnic of Central London in 1983. He established John Pardey Architects in 1988 and has since achieved 34 national and international awards.

John Pardey Architects have become nationally recognized. John was appointed as a member of CABE's National Design Review Panel in 2009.

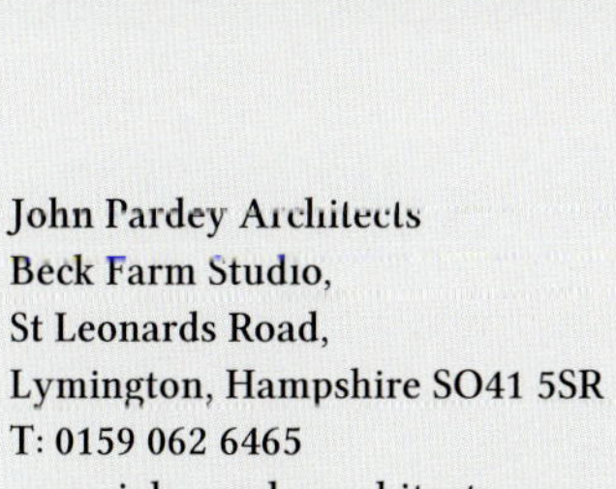

John Pardey Architects
Beck Farm Studio,
St Leonards Road,
Lymington, Hampshire SO41 5SR
T: 0159 062 6465
www.johnpardeyarchitects.com

The clients sought a forest retreat for short breaks, a holiday home that would be easy to use and maintain a strong connection to nature. This is a house that offers the opposite of day to day urban life, a place that breathes, is open and light, and offers an easy to maintain interaction with the immediate garden and the woodland that spills on beyond.

The sleek, timber clad box offers ample space that is well laid out. The master suite has been kept separate from the two bedrooms provided for the teenage children of the clients. There is also a distinct space for guests. However, a single social hub forms the heart of the home, offering space for cooking, eating and relaxing together.

The design arises from the idea of a simple, linear single-storey form that gently alights upon the ground. Two linear concrete foundations run along each side of the house, with a basement in the central section offering some additional space to the design. This base supports laminated timber floors, walls and the roof panels made from KLH timber. The panels, craned over the trees from the road, were erected in less than one week, and slender steel columns were employed to support the extensive glazed opening that faces into the woodland. The design tolerances of this system allowed for the windows to be pre-ordered, and the envelope of the home was weather-tight in a matter of weeks.

The striking external form is characterized by rigid insulation and a rainscreen of open jointed sweet chestnut slats over black mesh. The roof is a single ply membrane. The home in form and materiality communicates easily with the environment, creating a delightful dialogue with nature. The bedrooms face east, addressing the morning sun. The main living spaces and master bedroom suites face the woodland, offering a place to enjoy the changing seasons and to watch the sun set behind the trees.

Photography: James Morris

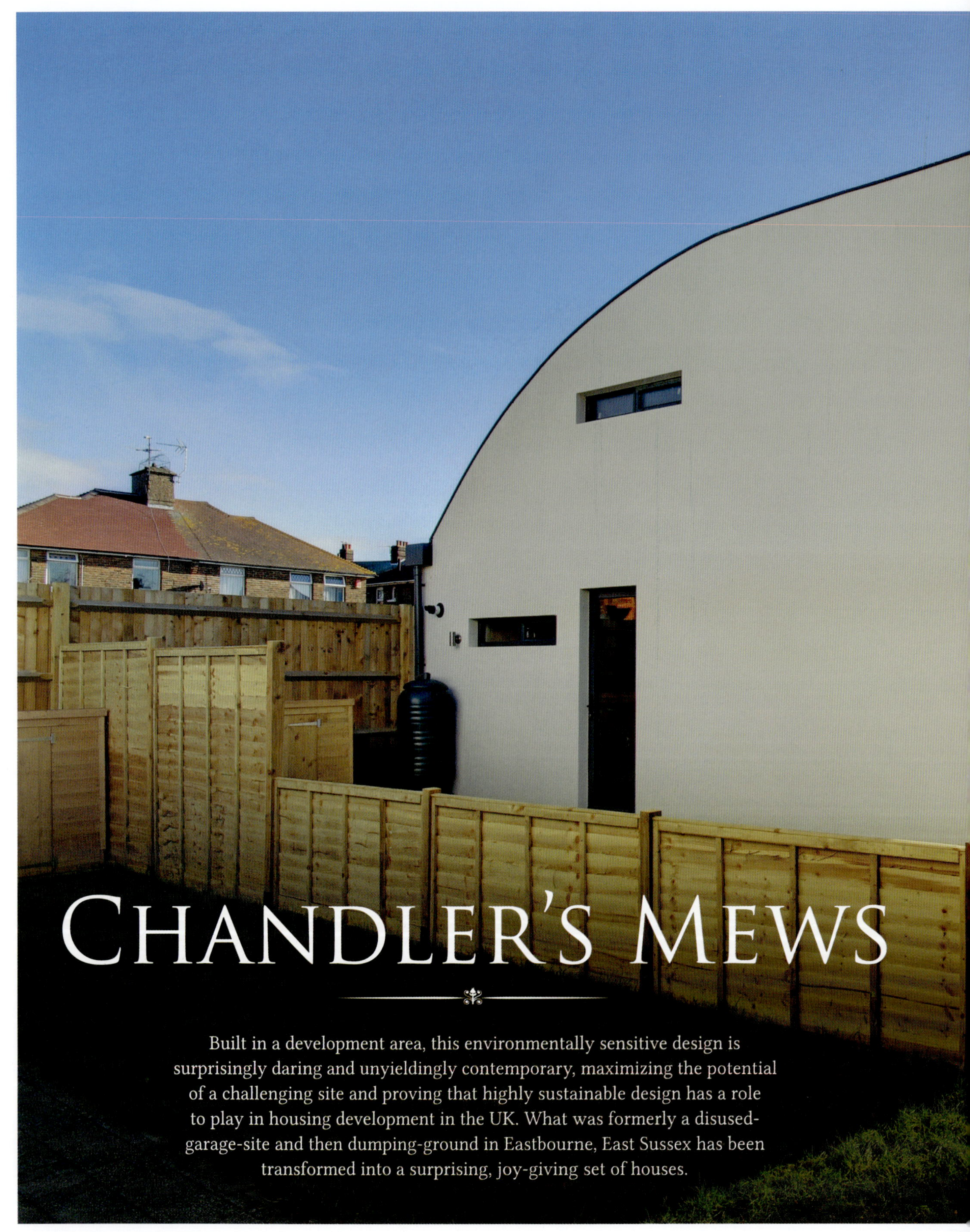

CHANDLER'S MEWS

Built in a development area, this environmentally sensitive design is
surprisingly daring and unyieldingly contemporary, maximizing the potential
of a challenging site and proving that highly sustainable design has a role
to play in housing development in the UK. What was formerly a disused-
garage-site and then dumping-ground in Eastbourne, East Sussex has been
transformed into a surprising, joy-giving set of houses.

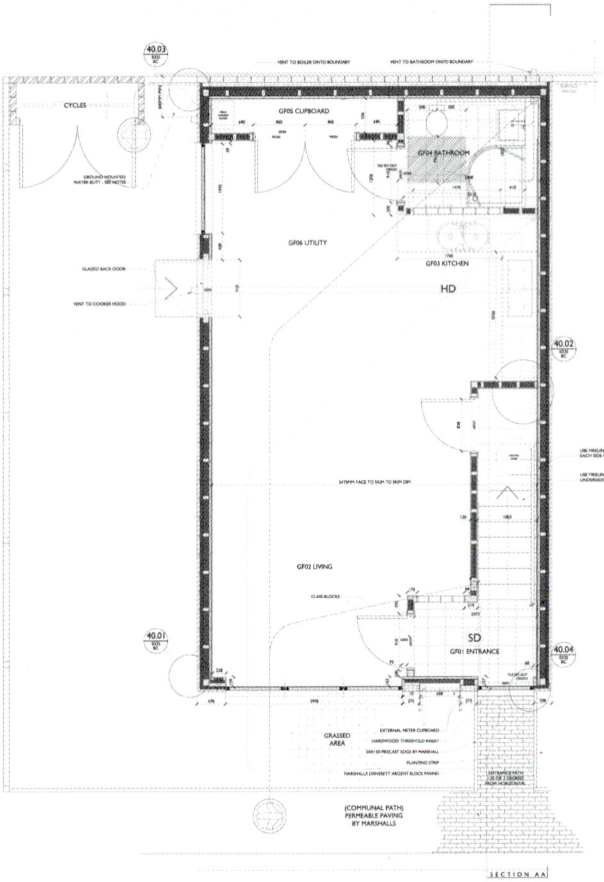

+00 **ground floor** plan - unit 1

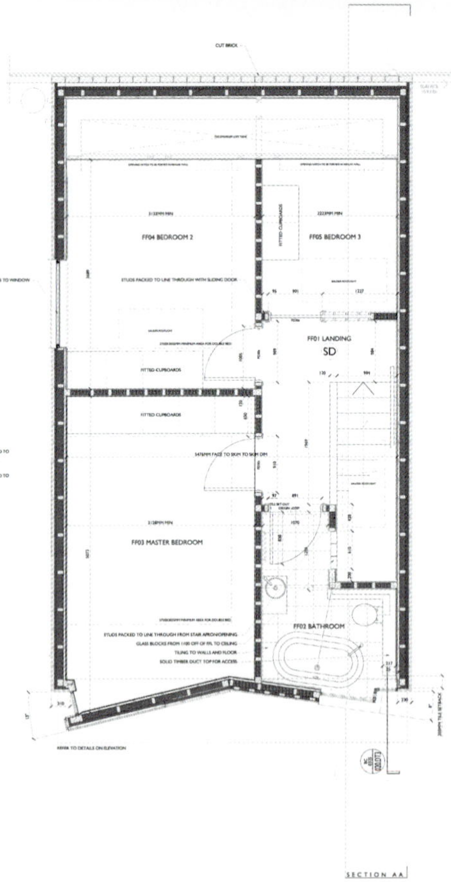

+01 **first floor** plan - unit 1

At 34, British born Architect Liam Russell works with his team of thirteen dedicated architects and designers to produce cost-effective yet highly conceptual, conscientious and sustainably designed buildings. Founded in 2007, the practice now works globally from a base in the UK, undertaking a variety of projects from residential housing to commercial leisure precincts and educational facilities.

Though this unflinchingly modern design has many notable elements, its bold yet uncomplicated form is its defining feature. The curved profile is both aesthetically arresting and practical, allowing for a full two storeys at the front of the property, which tapers to a single storey at the rear. This gives houses to the north a view of the Sedum-covered roofs, which, in contrast to the white render walls brings to mind the drastic chalk cliffs and rolling green hills of the South Downs in Sussex.

The form gives the houses a unique character, softening the impact of their bold design. Furthermore, it is key in helping the houses to assert their contemporary design – the form promotes the idea that modern houses, when completed with a sense of scale and place, can allow for the quirks of individual taste and decoration

The façade comprises a surprising juncture of materials, enhancing the visual impact of the home and complementing the strong yet simple design. White render on the sides and front of the property form a solid, grounding base to which recyclable powder-coated aluminium and FSC certified timber are a striking highlight. Brick plinths to the rear of the property provide a solid and robust backbone to the entire design, allowing movement and expansion without causing the building to degrade.

Sustainability and practicality are united in being central to this design. The FSC certified timber frame is super-insulated, and yet it has also been kept extremely thin to maximize the gross internal area. The Sedum roof, a striking visual feature, creates a micro-habitat that allows for rainwater attenuation, and the environmental pressure asserted by this home is further lessened by the use of solar thermal tubes built into the design.

Placed along the northernmost boundary of the development, these properties are afforded ample space for external amenities and a large internal space. Though the sites are relatively tight, the units are surprisingly spacious inside, with some visitors to the site remarking that the pods are 'TARDIS-like' inside.

Liam Russell Architects
The Studios,
3 Broad Reach Mews, Ropetackle,
Shoreham By Sea, BN43 5EY
T: 0845 180 3676
www.liamrussellarchitects.co.uk

Photography: Ben Harvey, Liam Russell Architects

THE SHADOW HOUSE

The Shadow House is a new build private house in Camden,
North London constructed as the primary residence of the architects
David Liddicoat and Sophie Goldhill.

First Floor

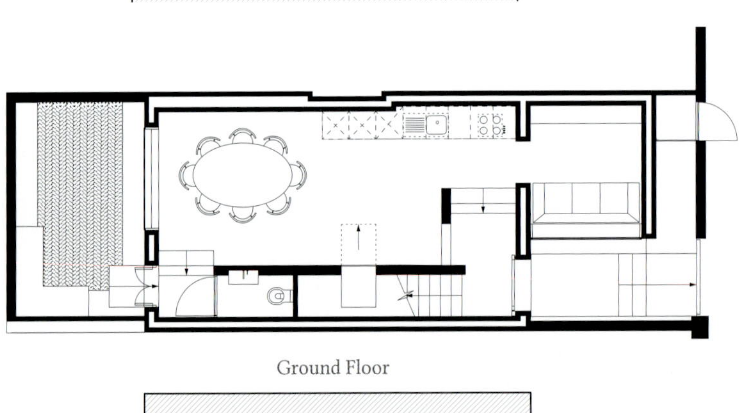

Ground Floor

David Liddicoat studied first at Cambridge University, while Sophie Goldhill trained at The Slade & Bartlett (UCL). David and Sophie met while at the Royal College of Art. Sophie began her career with Sir Norman Foster in London, while David worked for Daniel Libeskind in Berlin.

Experiencing the world of the 'starchitect' – a world of celebrity architects – led David and Sophie to eschew the flimsy formalism of the New Labour years that continue to obsess the profession. Instead, David and Sophie revel in the beauty of practical things and seek to make modest and characterful places to live.

David and Sophie established their practice with the express intention of designing and making houses; the Shadow House is their first completed new build home. They carried out the entire project themselves, from finding the site, through planning, design, construction and manufacture of the fittings, fixtures and furniture.

Liddicoat & Goldhill LLP
Studio 6,
13 Ramsgate Street,
London E8 2FD
T: 0207 923 2737
www.liddicoatgoldhill.com

The house, built inside and out of slim-format Dutch engineering brick with delicate black glaze, is situated on a scrap of land measuring only 38m2 formerly used as a parking garage. The tectonic of the house was driven by its physical and legislative context. The use of Dutch engineering brick, for instance, was informed by the input of Camden Planners, who felt that the house should reflect its tough industrial-era context. The result is a robust, monolithic design with an unforgiving monochromatic skin.

In order to give a sense of space to what would otherwise feel like constrained rooms, the designers felt it was important to be able to modulate the section and work with the heights. Different ceiling heights, adjusted by changes in the floor below and by different height roofs produce a range from 3m in the living room to 2.1m in the entrance area. This allowed each space to have its own temperature, sound quality and sense of coziness and airiness. There are certain knots of intensity, where the spatial and functional requirements of the house are tangled up.

One small luxury the designers allowed in their otherwise sparing design was two slabs of bookmatched Staturietto marble, which are used throughout the house as reflective contrast to the brick walls. The design revolves around this play of light and dark; carefully controlled moments of intensity and quiet shadow. The interior spaces are intense, controlled and quiet, creating maximum emotional effect.

Spaces are carved playfully into the walls to minimize everyday clutter. The television and cables are concealed behind a black glass wall, the toilet roll has its own marble niche, the washing machine is in a secret cupboard behind the toilet and discrete storage fills every spare corner while the kitchen extract is buried in the brickwork.

The architects, in the interests of turning their house into a space they could comfortably call home, designed their own fittings and furnishings. The Shadow Lamp for example is a granite and laser-cut timber table light that creates a warm ambience in the contrasting house.

The architects now live in the house, and are pleased with the sustainable outcomes achieved by the design. The building performs passively, minimizing the required heating load and eliminating the need for active ventilation. Stable thermal characteristics overcome the challenge of the tempering environment within a building with irregular occupancy.

Resembling a cut face of coal, the striking black is contrasted with sheer, frameless glazing with accents of white staurietto marble, echoing the plaster reveals and porticoes of the surrounding Victorian architecture. Simplicity and functionality combine to frame this house in the great poetry of practical things.

Photography: Tom Gildon & Keith Collie

GLASS HOUSE

A long, sinuous, reflective black wall introduces the home with a little mystery from the approach. Travelling along a gravel drive and through a wood toward the home, the sparse planting of trees gives away subtle glimpses of the sea as it begins to unravel an air of unique brilliance. At just a single level, the low profile of this coastal home affords a great degree of privacy, while offering sweeping views to the Solent beyond.

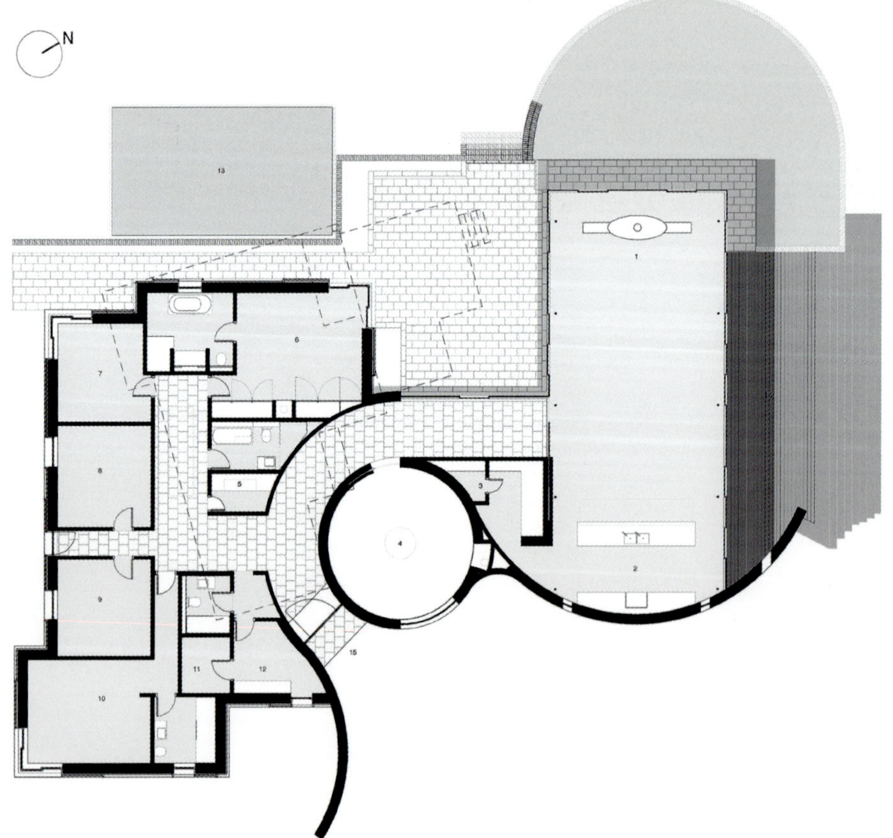

Floor Plan
1. Living Room
2. Kitchen
3. Pantry
4. Family Den
5. Bunk Room
6. Bedroom One
7. Bedroom Two
8. Bedroom Three
9. Bedroom Four
10. Bedroom Five
11. Plant Room
12. Utility Room
13. Swimming Pool
14. Pavilion Deck
15. Principal Entrance

Dotted lines indicate
position of former house.

Jonathan Manser comes from a family of architects, both his father and sister are architects, and his mother is an architectural journalist.

The family business, The Manser Practice, was formed by his father in the early 1960s and now has offices both in London and Leeds. With a work force of around 30, their projects have reached the world over. Jonathan is Managing Director.

He is regularly invited to act as an awards assessor, including judging for the RIBA and as European Hotel Design Awards Chairman of Judges.

The Manser Practice Architects & Designers
Bridge Studios,
107a Hammersmith Bridge Road,
Hammersmith, London W6 9DA
T: 0208 741 4381
www.manser.co.uk

A gorgeous oversized sawn timber door provides entry to the home – and you know from this point on that it's going to be special. Failing to disappoint, a restrained and mostly white palette provides a stunning sample of what to expect past the curved entry hall. Leading past a private family den you will arrive at the open plan pavilion which houses the kitchen and living area and make up one wing of the home.

Seemingly structureless, the pavillion appears to have no walls, with much of the perimeter clad in glass. This transparency affords a greater scale of light, as well as introducing vistas that few are lucky enough to experience. Glare is countered by the deep overhangs of the roof, also ensuring that the space is evenly lit and easier to comprehend in sunny weather, whilst being very well lit in more overcast conditions. The beautiful dark timber living room floor also absorbs solar gain, effectively reducing the load in the under-floor heating.

To the left of the entry corridor is the bedroom block, comprising five bedrooms and four bathrooms, as well as a plant and utility room. At the front of the property is a large entertaining area accompanied by a luxurious pool. Accessible from both wings of the home, this is an area that boasts astonishing views and the opportunity to utilise the surrounding land as an extension to its entertainment capabilities in the warmer months.

Upon consideration of the facts, The Manser Practice decided that rebuilding the existing home, rather than renovating, was more economical in the long run as it would allow for a more sustainably oriented approach to design.

Photography: Jonathan Manser and Morley von Sternberg

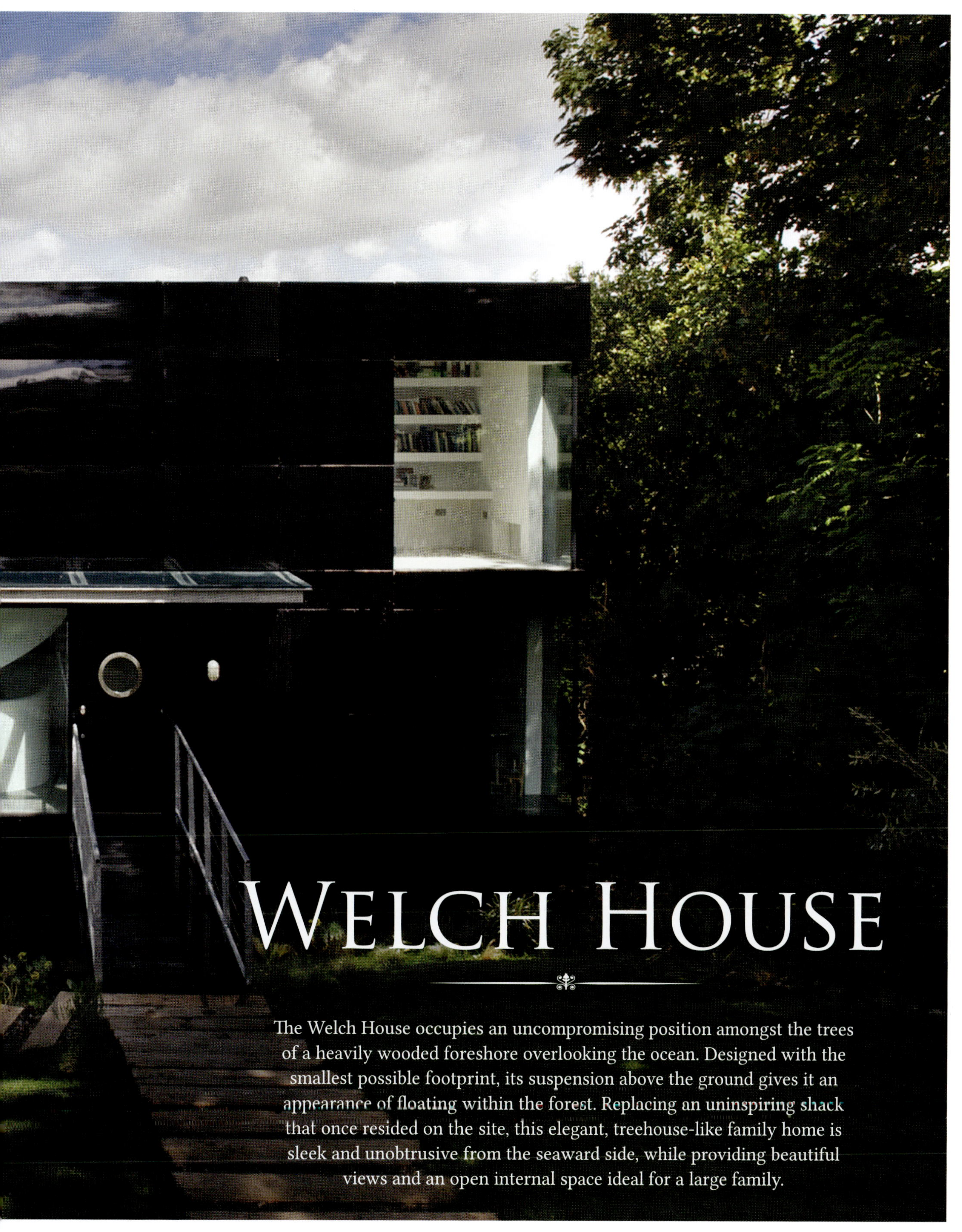

Welch House

The Welch House occupies an uncompromising position amongst the trees of a heavily wooded foreshore overlooking the ocean. Designed with the smallest possible footprint, its suspension above the ground gives it an appearance of floating within the forest. Replacing an uninspiring shack that once resided on the site, this elegant, treehouse-like family home is sleek and unobtrusive from the seaward side, while providing beautiful views and an open internal space ideal for a large family.

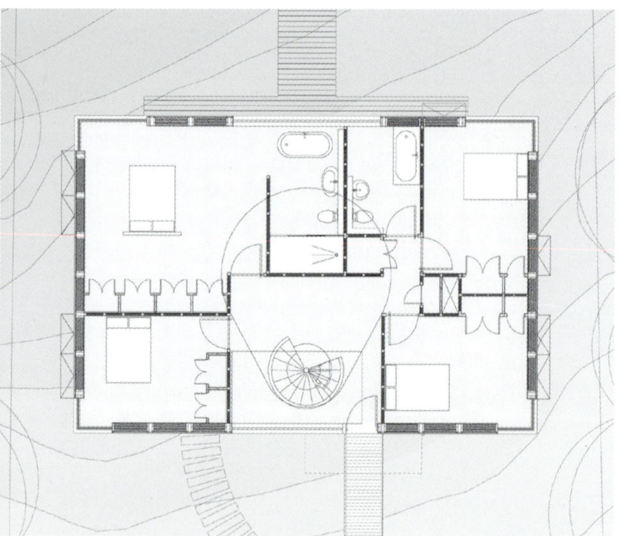

First Floor

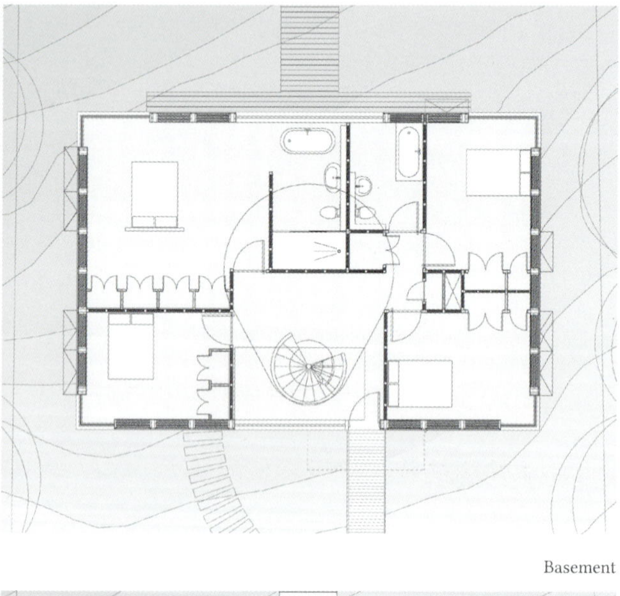

Ground Floor

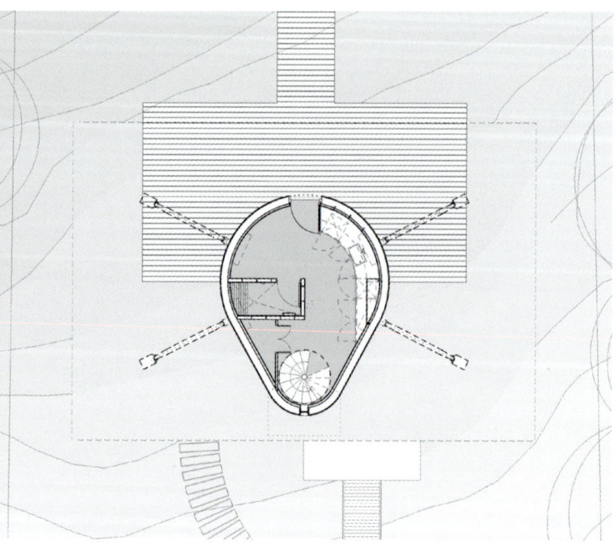

Basement

The complex site required substantial planning. A protracted planning application process involved research on the site going back to the middle of the 19th Century and long negotiations with the Environment Agency. The problems of physical construction on the site arise from the terrain – slippery clay on rotating shelves required foundations to be deeply piled and retained with soil nails. Overcoming the challenge, the complex concrete construction below ground ties the structure to a more stable bedrock below ground level.

The flat, polished surface of the exterior has its own unique beauty in form and strength. The rain screen cladding, with its marine high gloss enamel paint, provides a reflective surface onto which the surrounding trees are projected, allowing the building to blend gently into the environment.

The internal finishes are clean, simple and economic. All glazing is fixed, with ventilation and cross ventilation provided by a series of floor-level opening panels and roof lights. The tear-shaped concrete dupe beneath the floating box contains a utility room and shower room, balancing the entrance and bedrooms on the ground floor and the expansive living and kitchen area and study on the first floor.

Efficient gas-fired central heating serves underfloor elements within the heavily insulated building. Combined with the economic use of ventilation for cooling, this arrangement gives the clients the most practical solution for thermal control.

Simplicity and efficiency ensure the success of this home. Rather than competing with the striking physical beauty of such a rich site, the home seeks to merge and reflect with it, overcoming site challenges to hover comfortably amongst the trees.

Photography: Jonathan Manser and Morley von Sternberg

The Manser Practice Architects & Designers
Bridge Studios,
107a Hammersmith Bridge Road,
Hammersmith, London W6 9DA
T: 0208 741 4381
www.manser.co.uk

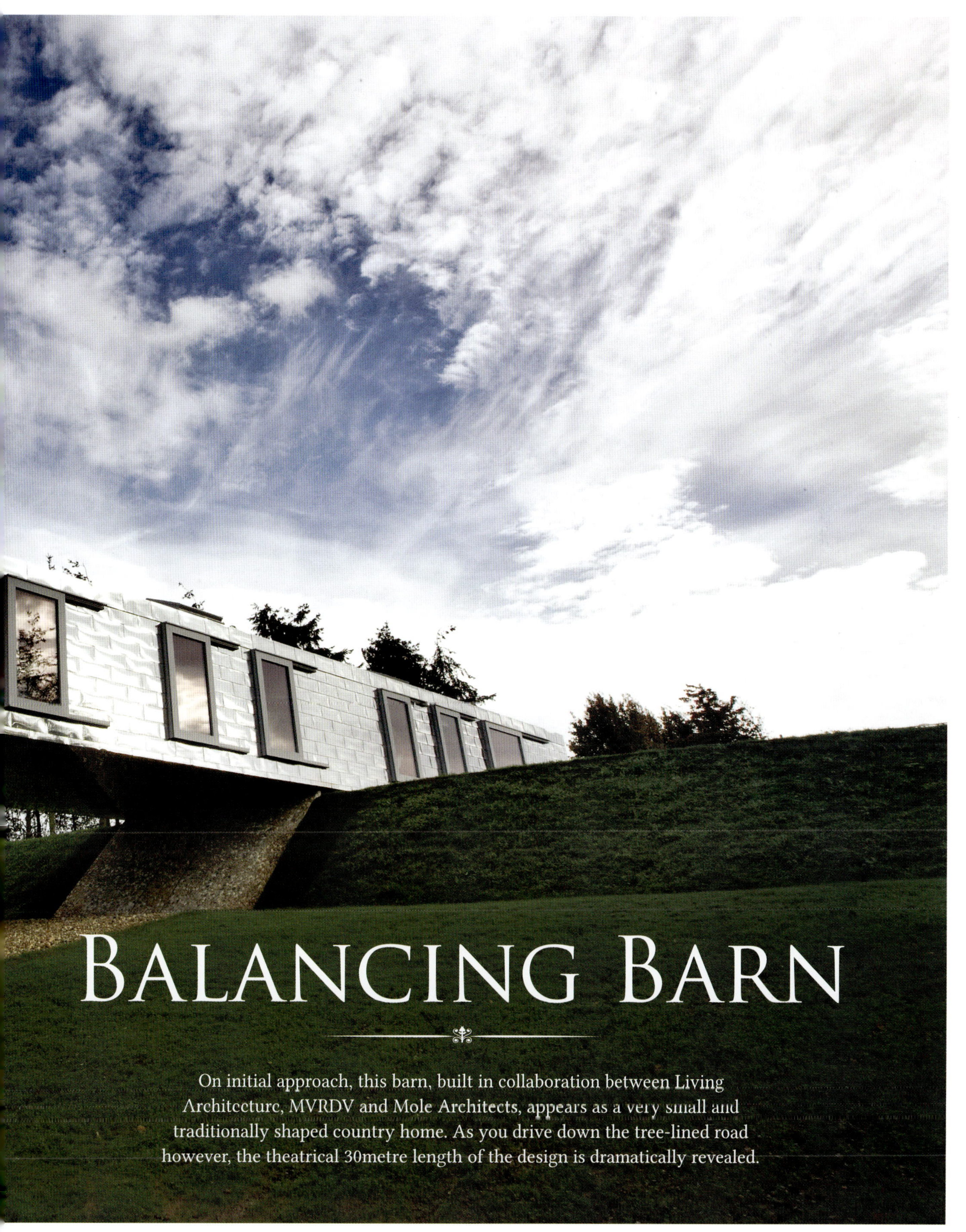

BALANCING BARN

On initial approach, this barn, built in collaboration between Living
Architecture, MVRDV and Mole Architects, appears as a very small and
traditionally shaped country home. As you drive down the tree-lined road
however, the theatrical 30metre length of the design is dramatically revealed.

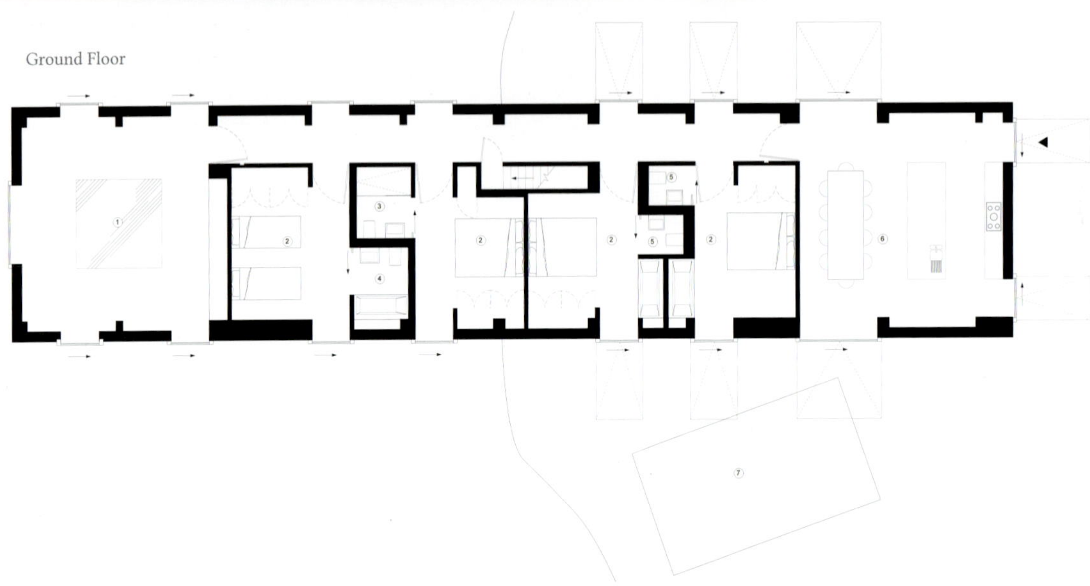

Ground Floor

Basement

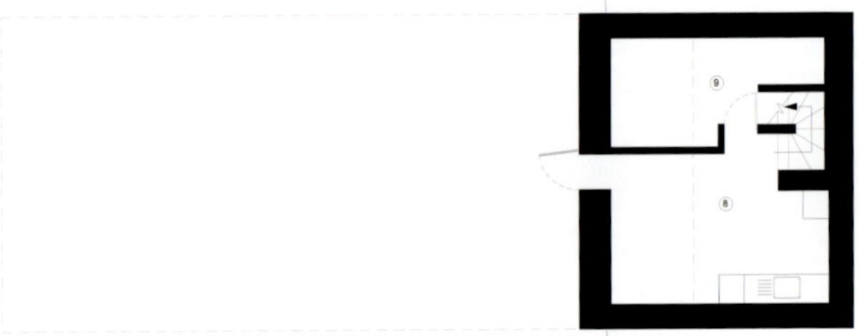

Legend
1 Living room
2 Bedroom
3 En-suite Shower room
4 En-suite bathrom
5 W/C
6 Kitchen
7 High terrace
8 Basement Utility
9 Mechanical Room

Winy Maas

The architecture practice MVRDV was set up in Rotterdam, Netherlands, in 1993 by Winy Maas, Jacob van Rijs and Nathalie de Vries. Working in close collaboration, the three principal architects produce designs for cities, individual buildings and landscapes. MVRDV has an interest in simple, down-to-earth solutions that nevertheless have a great sense of humour and humanity about them. They have done much in the field of social housing and have worked to create an entirely new standard for this category.

Meredith Bowles

Meredith Bowles is the founder and principal of Mole Architects Ltd., based in Ely, Cambridgeshire, a firm that has established itself as a leading practice for designing low-energy, contemporary buildings with a particular emphasis on regional character. In addition, Mole Architects have collaborated with international practices MVRDV, Jarmund Vigsnaes, and UK based architect Peter Salter.

Mole Architects
Babylon Bridge,
Waterside, Ely CB7 4AU
T: 0135 366 7068
www.molearchitects.co.uk

The site, formerly known as Church Farm and owned by the Suffolk Wildlife Trust, previously contained an unremarkable 1950s bungalow and large garage, along with a number of derelict buildings and barns. Due to the environmental sensitivity of the site, Living Architecture undertook a programme of mitigation for the careful removal of protected species before starting building works. The undergrowth was cleared and a large number of non-local tree species removed in order to return the site to its natural state and reveal the stunning potential of the location.

Upon completion of this task, Living Architecture turned to the Dutch Firm MVRDV for guidance on the site. Together, they eventually decided that a balancing structure was an obvious, if not easily executed way to exploit the dramatic level variation of the site. The resulting 15 metre cantilever, which is half the length of the entire structure, gives one the feeling of being suspended above the natural landscape, an impression reinforced by a glass floor and ceiling in the sitting room.

The façade has been kept texturally simple, with small hints of the structural requirements visible through the windows. On the inside however, the timber-lined surfaces fold around the steel beams, creating complex angles and shapes. Both the exterior and interior are finished with one material in a continuous skin, which gives a pleasing visual continuity to the home. The exterior mirrored cladding (polished stainless steel) reflects the house's surroundings and helps it blend in, while the interior is lined with sheets of ash faced plywood, the surface only 'broken' by alcoves or cupboards.

The internal spaces are simply defined. A substantial kitchen and dining room, with large sliding windows, leads to a long corridor that spans the length of the house. Branching off from this corridor are four bedrooms, each with its own bathroom. In particular, two of the bedrooms have 'in room' baths, something that MVRDV was keen to include from the outset. At the far end of the house is a large sitting room with huge picture windows to immerse inhabitants in the surrounding landscape. A semi-concealed door located off the corridor gives access, via a staircase, to the garden below.

Photography: Chris Wright, Living Architecture

CAVENDISH

The scale and form of this design is influenced by the eclectic and diverse streetscape of Cavendish Avenue - a tree-lined suburban enclave that is rich in architectural character and domestic diversity. Replacing an existing 1930s detached house, this new home is a similarly unique, economically passive and sustainable villa.

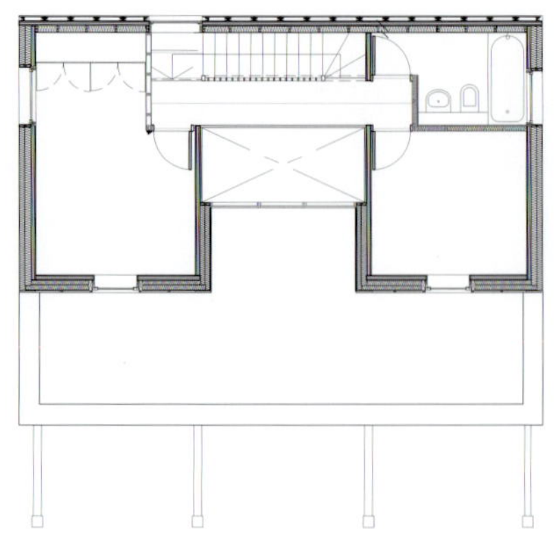

Second Floor

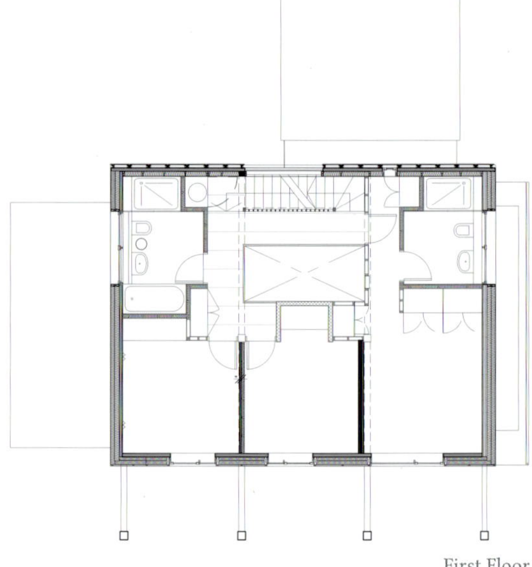

First Floor

Ground Floor

The previous house on the site was a crude amalgamation of modernist aesthetic and traditional rural cottage style. The interior was uncomfortable and cramped, and within its context it provided only a series of small, unfriendly spaces. In replacing the existing building, the new villa provides a dwelling zone of consummate quality. Design, scale and construction have been undertaken as a unified process, reinforcing and merging with the existing overall architectural quality of the street.

Taking cues from the streetscape, the villa is large in scale and sits well back from the road. The layout, on the other hand, employs the German Passivhaus standards for energy efficiency. The form is a direct response to passive solar design, with solar gain offered through the north-south orientation of the site. Further, the ground floor and projecting room are clad in timber, while the first and second floor façades are made up of a rain-screen composed of semi-reflective fritted glass in front of an insulated panel. This provides a reflective, opaque skin, avoiding a corporate feel through the use of small glass panels, which add a touch of delicacy to the bold façade.

At the opposite end of the building, a large glazed area is located on the southern façade, opening out to the garden. Large panel sliding glass doors sit behind timber screens, masking the structural columns and acting as sun shades. Screens to the side of the home also prevent overlooking from the property, while openings to the north are limited to three windows, the largest of which is situated opposite the living room and central stair.

The interior is aesthetically sympathetic to the outside of the home and draws visual inspiration from the simple materials of the passive solar design. The exposed timber and natural light give the space a fresh, comfortable, simple air that the previous home on the site lacked.

While the house was initially contentious at the planning stage, the Council Planning department now use it as an example of how contemporary design can work in existing historic neighbourhoods, providing a framework for the evolution of architecture in Britain's heritage areas.

Photography: David Butler

Mole Architects
Babylon Bridge,
Waterside, Ely CB7 4AU
T: 0135 366 7068
www.molearchitects.co.uk

DUNE HOUSE

The Dune House in Thorpeness on the Suffolk Coast bears a
strong relationship to the form of traditional British seaside
strip houses, while drawing in a new contemporary materiality.
In this eclectic vacation destination, this stunning beach
design balances environmental concerns and conservation area
requirements with a commitment to excellent architecture.

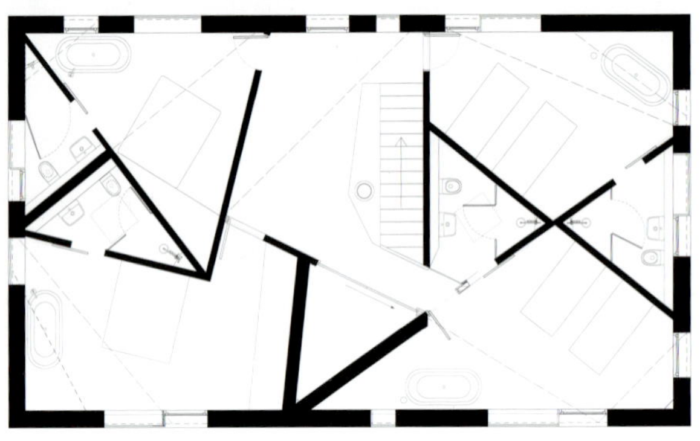

First Floor

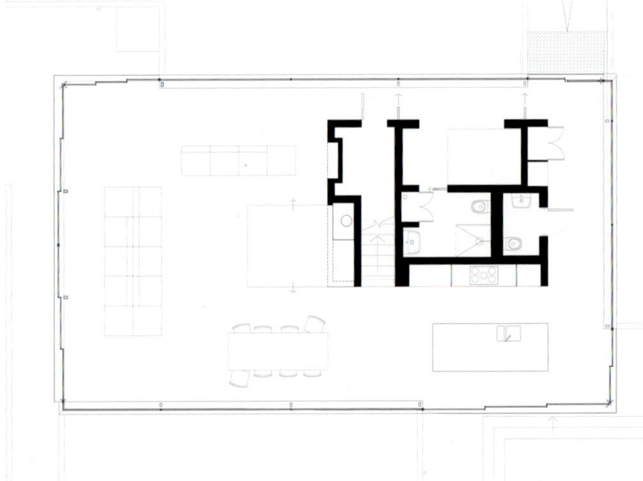

Ground Floor

Håkon Vigsnæs

JVA, established in 1996, is a young Norwegian practice responsible for building a series of highly accomplished, modestly-priced houses in Oslo and its outskirts. Past projects include working with the Norwegian Ministry of Defence in 2006, Galleri Trafo (Norway) in 2006 and the Oslo School of Architecture in 2002.

The client, Living Architecture, selected Jarmund Vigsnaes Arkitekter through a short competition process to design a replacement for the two-storey chalet bungalow previously found on this site, one of the only inhabited stretches of beach in England, while Mole Architects were appointed as collaborators as part of their ongoing relationship with the client. The new home was to be the second in a series of redevelopments for Living Architecture, with others designed by Nord, David Kohn and Peter Zumthor. The previous house had been extended upon ad hoc during its 100 year lifetime and was suffering serious structural problems. The new home was to be built on the existing footprint to offer a romantic remembrance to holidays at bed and breakfasts.

Located on the edge of a conservation space in an area of outstanding natural beauty, consultation with planning officers throughout the design and development process was integral to gaining support for the project. This diligent attention to the requirements of the build ensured that the house had full backing from the planning committee upon submission of the design.

The ground floor is a stunning glazed box. Set into the dunes to protect it from the strong winds, and equally to open it in all directions for wide views, it gives the solid wood clad top floor the appearance of floating above the sand. Additionally, the corners of this level can be opened as sliding doors, emphasising the flowing accessibility.

The geometrically complex first floor and roof are constructed from cross-laminated timber panels supplied by Eurban. Concrete, glass and aluminium on the ground level relate the mass to the ground, while the upper floor is constructed in solid wood, with the cladding stained dark to match the existing gables and sheds found in the area. This juxtaposition of light and dark creates a vibrant contrast between the ground and first floors.

Given the 1 in 200 year risk of flooding, the home's design makes some concessions. The polished concrete and easily removable doors found on the ground floor are two such examples of how the issue of flooding was accounted for. In addition, the house has a central core of concrete situated upon a raft foundation, while the first floor is supported by slender steel posts that rely on the concrete spine, which also contains the stairs, plant room, water closet and shower rooms.

Photography: Chris Wright, Living Architecture

Mole Architects
Babylon Bridge,
Waterside, Ely CB7 4AU
T: 0135 366 7068
www.molearchitects.co.uk

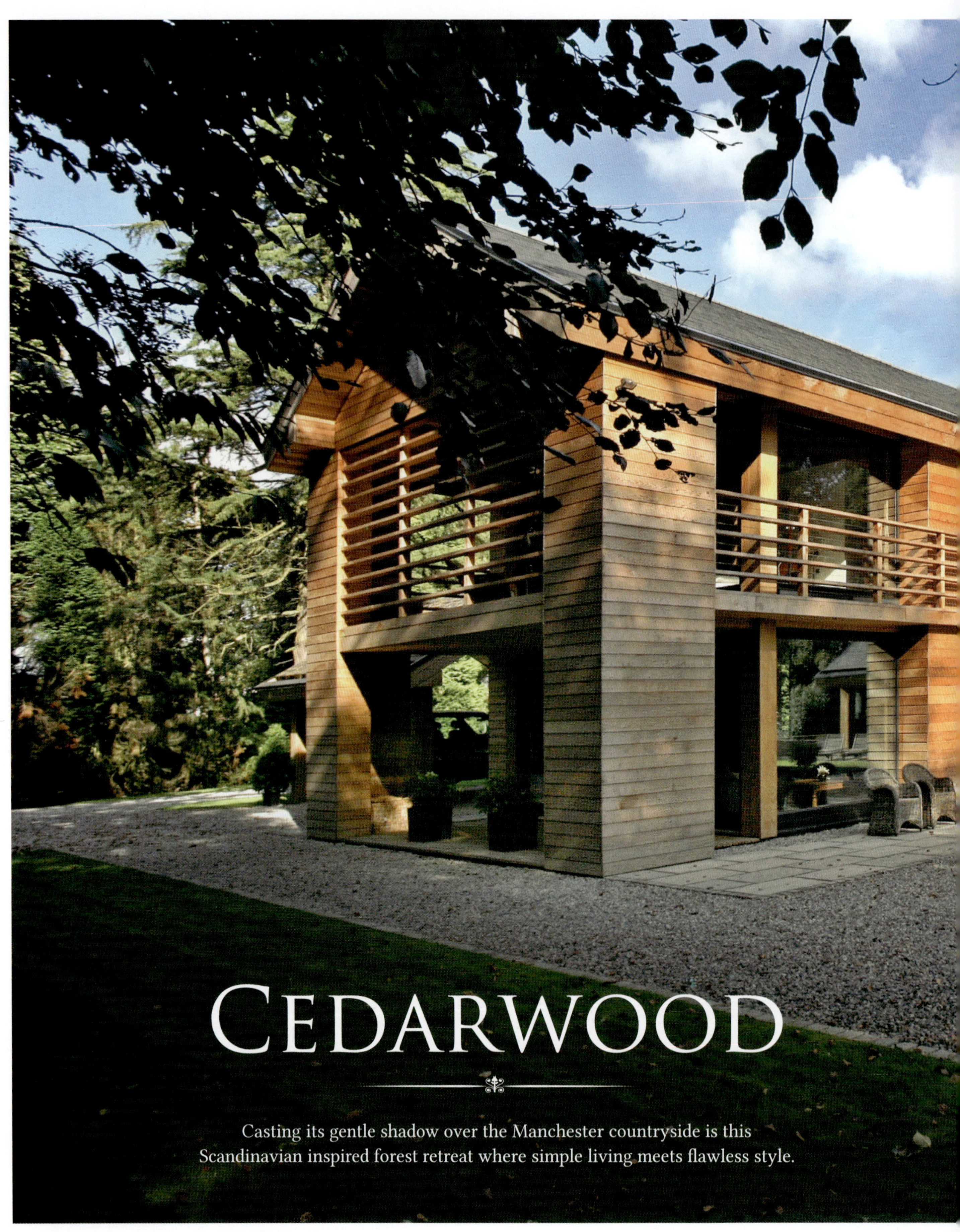

CEDARWOOD

Casting its gentle shadow over the Manchester countryside is this
Scandinavian inspired forest retreat where simple living meets flawless style.

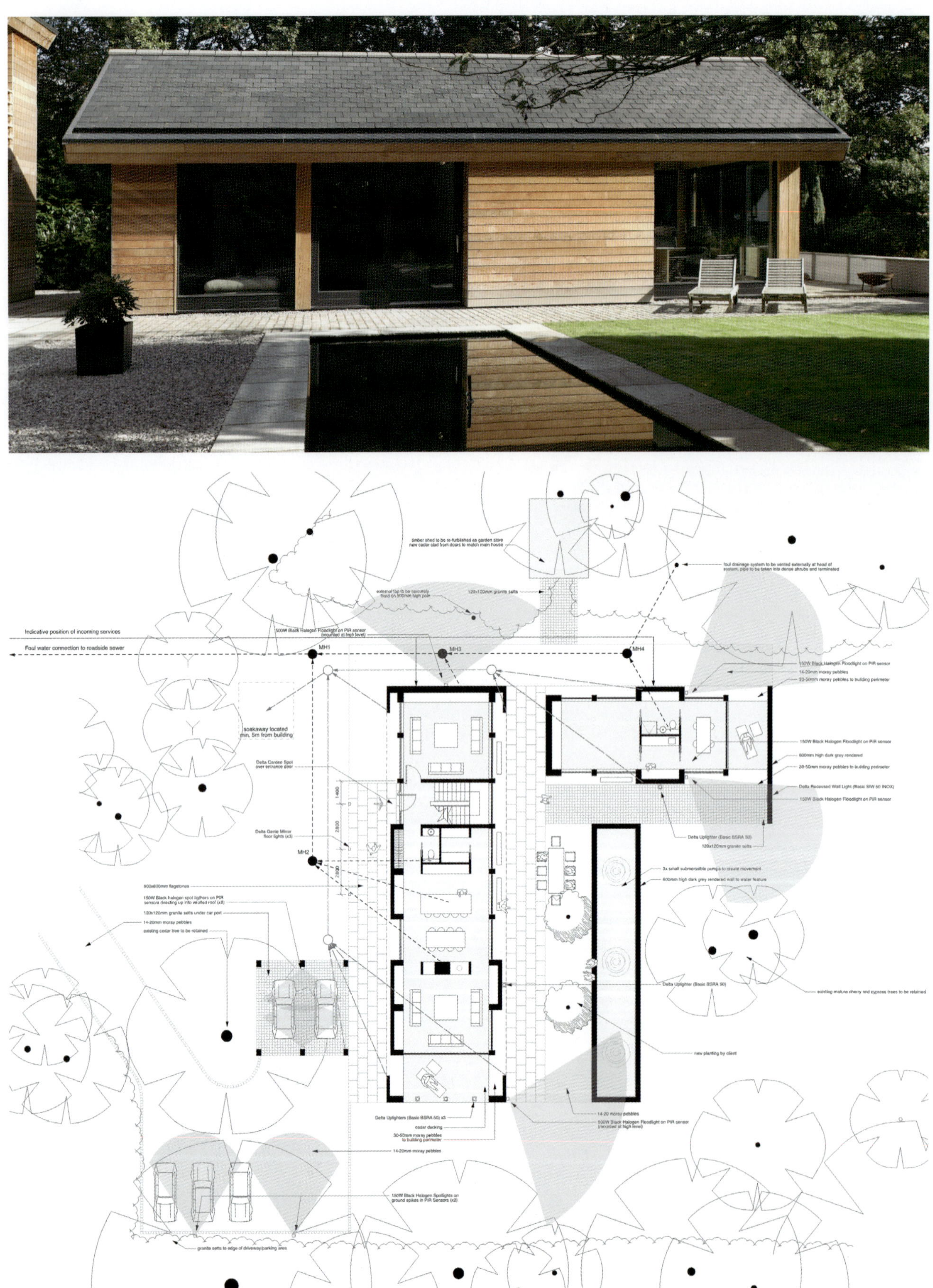

timber shed to be re-furbished as garden store
new cedar clad front doors to match main house
foul drainage system to be vented externally at head of
system, pipe to be taken into dense shrubs and terminated
external tap to be securely
fixed on 900mm high pole
120x120mm granite setts
Indicative position of incoming services
500W Black Halogen Floodlight on PIR sensor
(mounted at high level)
Foul water connection to roadside sewer
150W Black Halogen Floodlight on PIR sensor
14-20mm moray pebbles
30-50mm moray pebbles to building perimeter
MH1
MH3
MH4
soakaway located
min. 5m from building
150W Black Halogen Floodlight on PIR sensor
600mm high dark grey rendered
30-50mm moray pebbles to building perimeter
Delta Centro Spot
over entrance door
Delta Recessed Wall Light (Basic SW 50 INOX)
150W Black Halogen Floodlight on PIR sensor
Delta Genie Mirror
floor lights (x3)
Delta Uplighter (Basic BSRA 50)
120x120mm granite setts
MH2
3x small submersible pumps to create movement
600mm high dark grey rendered wall to water feature
900x600mm flagstones
150W Black halogen spot lighters on PIR
sensors directing up into vaulted roof (x2)
120x120mm granite setts under car port
14-20mm moray pebbles
existing cedar tree to be retained
Delta Uplighter (Basic BSRA 50)
existing mature cherry and cypress trees to be retained
new planting by client
14-20 moray pebbles
Delta Uplighters (Basic BSRA 50) x3
cedar decking
500W Black Halogen Floodlight on PIR sensor
(mounted at high level)
30-50mm moray pebbles to
building perimeter
14-20mm moray pebbles
150W Black Halogen Spotlights on
ground spikes in PIR Sensors (x2)
granite setts to edge of driveway/parking area

Training at both North London University and University College London, Nicolas Tye developed his unique approach to architecture and design through years of education, as well as practical training in his father's studio, Alan Tye Design, and ORMS Architects in Clerkenwell.

In 2004, after a number of years in the ORMS London office, Nicolas had the opportunity to buy a derelict 2500 sq ft barn in Bedfordshire. Wishing to understand more about the hands-on issues of building, Nicolas took a year out of his role as a project architect to build his own house. In doing so, he learned how to site manage, coordinate and complete a project beyond the traditional architect's understanding.

Nicolas Tye Architects
The Long Barn Studio,
Limbersey Lane,
Maulden, Bedfordshire MK45 2EA
T: 0152 540 6677
www.nicolastyearchitects.com

Lovingly embraced by a lush, mature landscape, this environmentally responsive country home by innovative architect Nicolas Tye is a dreamy abode all throughout the year.

The surrounding woodland environment presented an interesting challenge as to where to build, and saw the design evolve into a series of simple structures that reflect the surrounding landscape. Pale pavers and loose pebbles bridge said landscape to the timber and glass house that appears to float across the land. Modern and contemporary with a relaxed refinement, the structures adopt the always chic Scandinavian aesthetic that the design savvy clients desired.

Challenging the notion that simple means boring, the linear building form is a masterpiece in low maintenance, robust materials, making just the right impression without overpowering the real feature – nature.

The home's interior speaks a subtle elegance, with slick, smooth finishes and modern furniture. Spreading across the bottom floor, the main living areas enjoy an easy continuity, with slight definition achieved with the stack stone, double-sided fire place that marks the lounge. Similarly warmed by the fire, the dining area and kitchen express a slightly more striking identity with bright whites contrasting charcoal features.

Partial height walls bring the grandeur of the cathedral ceiling into the first floor spaces. From the master bedroom, the roof form continues out onto a semi enclosed balcony where timber slats and a timber clad roof provide a cozy haven for year round enjoyment.

Semi-frosted glass provides just the right amount of privacy to the chic and modern bathrooms, allowing for the experience of the rural atmosphere within a warm and inviting room that maintains a modern aesthetic.

A serene place to relax and take in the quiet of nature, the garden is made particularly alluring with a linear water feature that runs the length of the house. Sitting to one end is a quaint guesthouse that frames the garden court. Mimicking the main house in materials and design intention, the guesthouse opens widely to the garden and is stylishly furnished creating a cozy little abode for guest stays.

Everything about the home speaks a rural vernacular with a stylish and contemporary accent; from the way glazing integrates the inside with the out to the way timber cladding embraces the gorgeous green outlook. Country sensitive architecture realized to its full potential, this home is a jewel in the crown of architect Nicholas Tye.

Photography provided by Nicolas Tye Architects

DOVECOTE BARN

Finding luxury in simplicity and forming a sympathetic, complementary addition to a Heritage property, this rear extension to Dovecote Barn designed by George Yam and Nicolas Tye has transformed the building into a practical family living space. Adding depth to the long, narrow footprint of the existing construct, the addition contains new dining and informal social areas, providing direct access and a strong visual link to the main living and children's play areas. In addition, the secondary objective of retaining the character of the building has also been achieved.

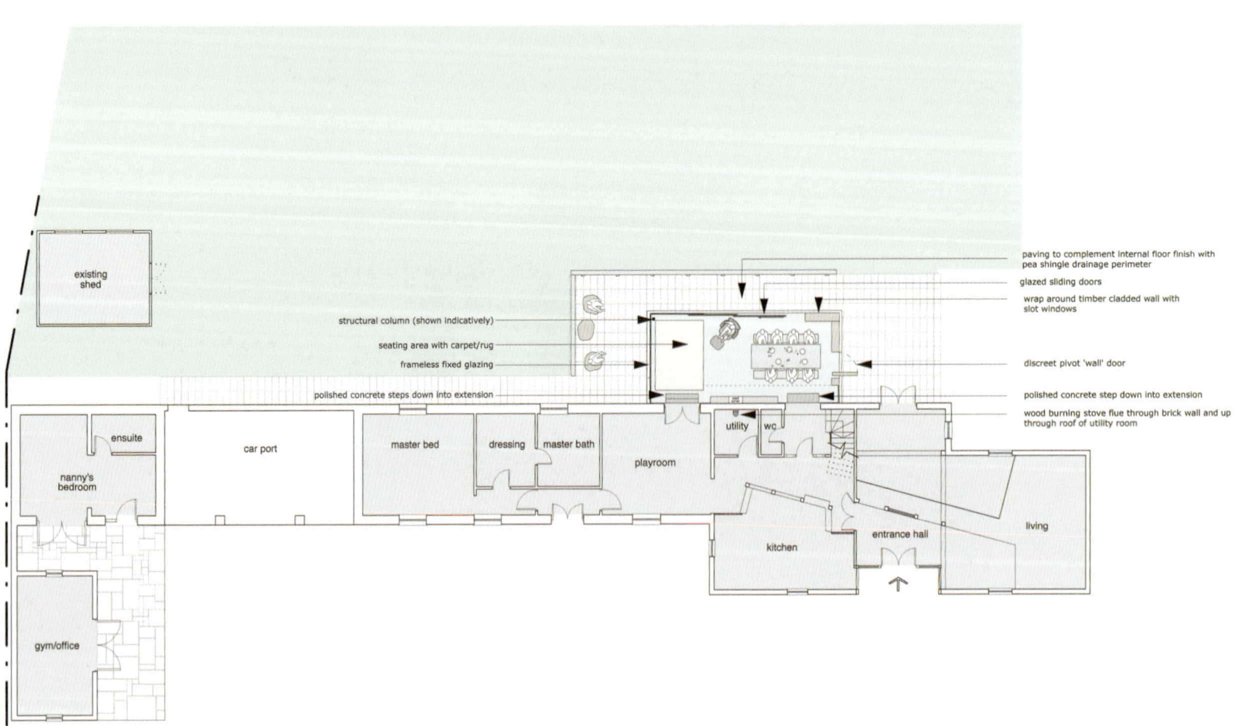
existing
shed
structural column (shown indicatively)
seating area with carpet/rug
frameless fixed glazing
polished concrete steps down into extension
paving to complement internal floor finish with pea shingle drainage perimeter
glazed sliding doors
wrap around timber cladded wall with slot windows
discreet pivot 'wall' door
polished concrete step down into extension
wood burning stove flue through brick wall and up through roof of utility room
ensuite
nanny's bedroom
gym/office
car port
master bed
dressing
master bath
playroom
utility
wc
kitchen
entrance hall
living

Located in Great Amwell, Hertfordshire, Dovecote Barn is found within a local conservation area. As such, a major challenge lay in getting the local authority to accept such a contemporary addition within the historical region. Fortunately, detailed research into the heritage frontage of the barn, in addition to pre-planning advice sought from the Conservation and Planning Offices, ensured that the proposed design would satisfy both the council and the owners. Additionally, the local Parish Council and owners of seven neighbouring properties were consulted, with all giving unanimous support for the scheme from the planning stage.

The existing barn is the true statement of the exterior, with its relationship to the extension playing a key role in the aesthetic impact of the façade. The design respects the heritage of the old building, retaining the strong linear aspect of the existing property. In addition, the profile has been 'tucked under' the existing eave level, so as to minimise the visual impact. Full height glazed panels were strategically placed to highlight the exposed brick wall of the barn and the views out to the landscaped garden. Native plants were used in the landscaping to further integrate the building into its setting.

The extensive glazing located on two sides of the extension allow the existing building fabric to appear as a feature of the design and provide a sense of lightness in the structure. With its new dining area, the addition has allowed the existing dining room in the original home to be converted into a children's play space, which is both visible and accessible from the current main living space. Level access is provided for a seamless transition from inside to out.

There is an elegant, simple luxury to this extension that arises from its finishes and products. Hand batched polished concrete flooring and steps are a solid, cool and neutral flooring option, underneath which a Nu Heat single zone underfloor heating system provides climate control. Allgood door furniture brings a subtle elegance to every room, while the Sonos built-in audio system is one of those little indulgences that is so often overlooked, yet so integral in characterising a space. Modular lighting with Rako controls complete the extension's interior makeup.

Nicolas Tye Architects
The Long Barn Studio,
Limbersey Lane,
Maulden, Bedfordshire MK45 2EA
T: 0152 540 6677
www.nicolastyearchitects.com

Photography: Nerida Howard

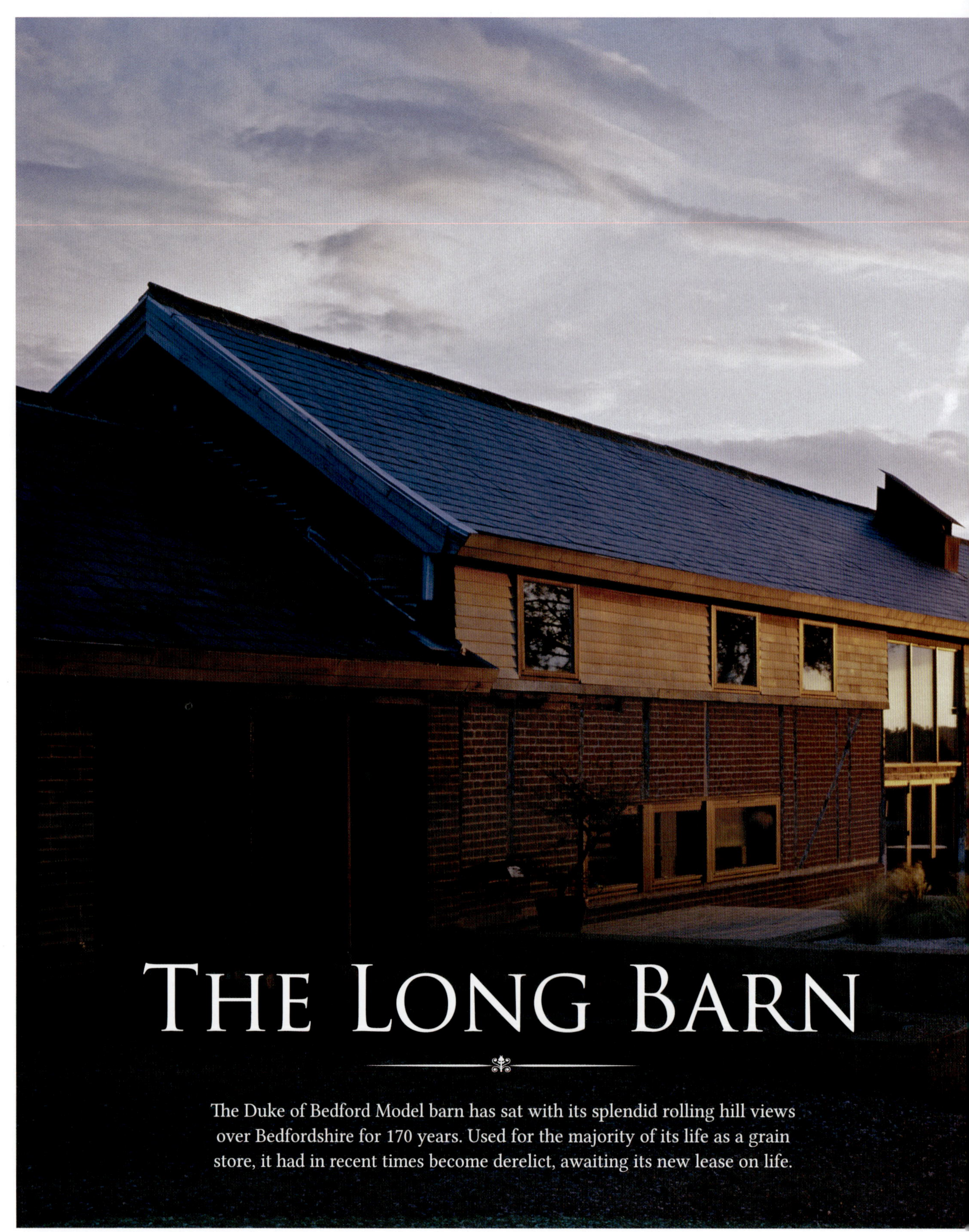

The Long Barn

The Duke of Bedford Model barn has sat with its splendid rolling hill views over Bedfordshire for 170 years. Used for the majority of its life as a grain store, it had in recent times become derelict, awaiting its new lease on life.

Constructed from oak and local bricks, this 40 metre long, six metre wide barn exuding beauty and charming character was converted into a home by the talented team at Nicolas Tye Architects.

The original 275 square metres the barn covered was increased to 387 square metres by the slight excavation of the ground floor, and the addition of a new first floor. Now an impressive two and a half stories high, the barn achieves a graceful balance between interacting levels.

As one approaches the barn from the west, the six by six metre fully glazed gable end makes a stunning statement. This due west glazed elevation receives dramatic views of rolling countryside as well as panoramic evening sunsets.

The property is framed by a metre high solid wall punctuated only by a single circle offering a glimpse to the landscape beyond. Raised garden beds planted with native grasses step down the length of the house alongside a timber deck.

A garage and studio sit at the higher end of the barn on one level, half way between the ground and first floors to the main building. Here, steps lead down to the entrance which has a cortan steel canopy and entrance grid which harps back to the agricultural era. A modernist glazed five metre high entrance sits behind in respect of the original elevation. This allows light to flood into the entrance hall which divides work and living areas.

Once inside, the chic and contemporary interior is breathtaking. The existing roof – a series of elm trusses emanating off a member running the length of the barn – is a spectacular feature. The first floor enjoys the glory of the original roof up close, whilst certain areas of the ground floor open expansively upward to create generous spaces.

Although open plan, the feeling of the interior is not one of starkness, as the integration of spaces is gently punctuated by elements that give subdivision and indeed intimacy to certain areas. For example, a two metre wide stack stone fireplace is an eye-catching feature that warms both floors, visually and functionally. Similarly, the stepping down of spaces to the ground floor neatly gives a sense of enclosure though the rooms remain open.

A cantilevering cortan steel stair reaches up to the first floor, where four bedrooms and two bathrooms are connected via a floating bridge. Windows in each bedroom throw the eye out to the views of open landscape and the lake.

Set back from the rural road on some six acres, this lovingly restored and renovated barn acts as a beacon atop the hill – especially when lit up at night. The majestic home, sympathetically combining old and new is a cohesive and intriguing design that epitomises rural living.

Nicolas Tye Architects
The Long Barn Studio,
Limbersey Lane,
Maulden, Bedfordshire MK45 2EA
T: 0152 540 6677
www.nicolastyearchitects.com

Photography provided by Nicolas Tye Architects

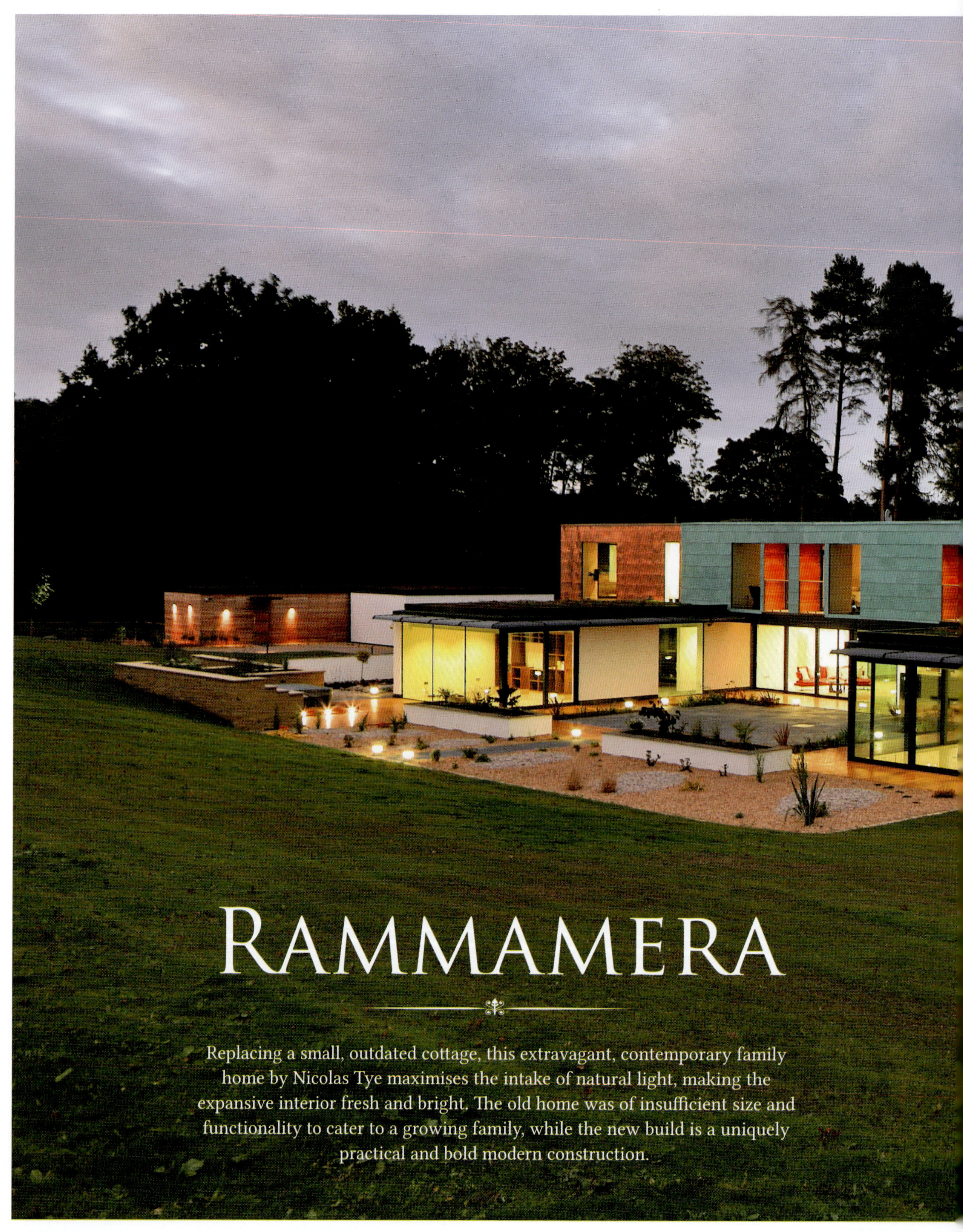

RAMMAMERA

Replacing a small, outdated cottage, this extravagant, contemporary family home by Nicolas Tye maximises the intake of natural light, making the expansive interior fresh and bright. The old home was of insufficient size and functionality to cater to a growing family, while the new build is a uniquely practical and bold modern construction.

First Floor

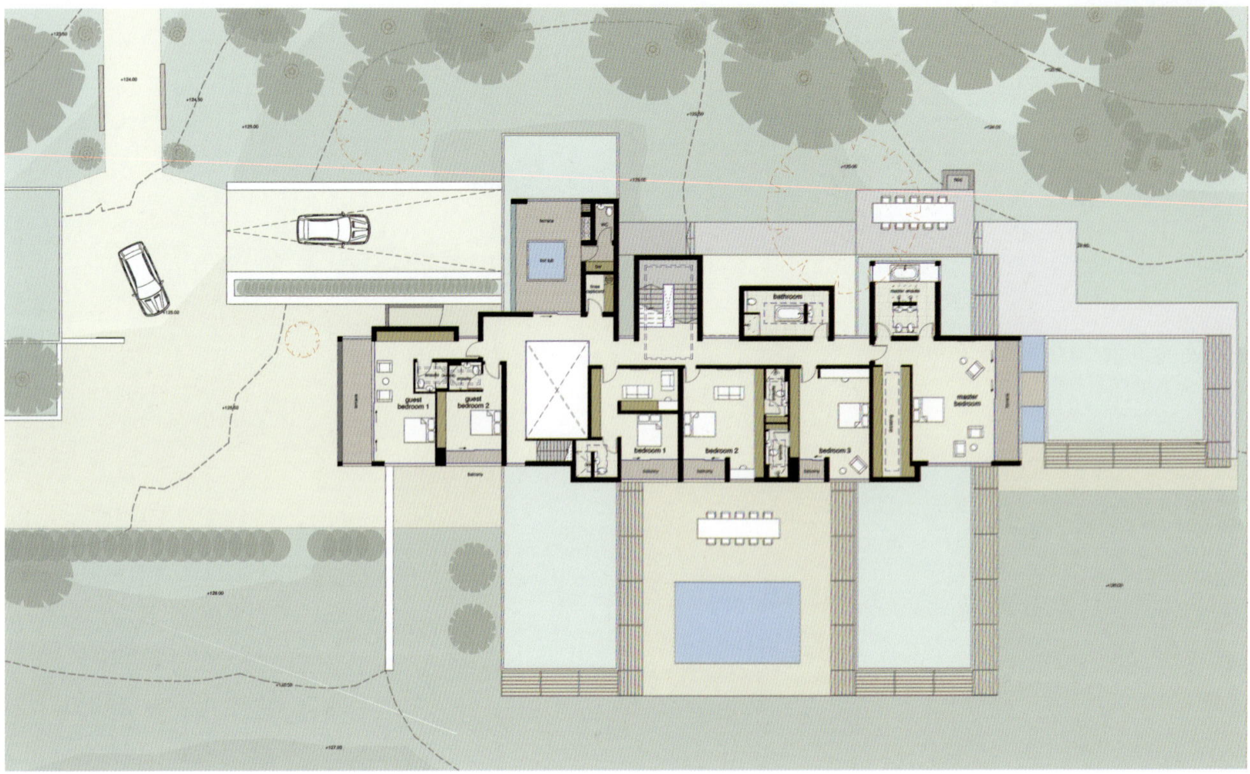

Ground Floor

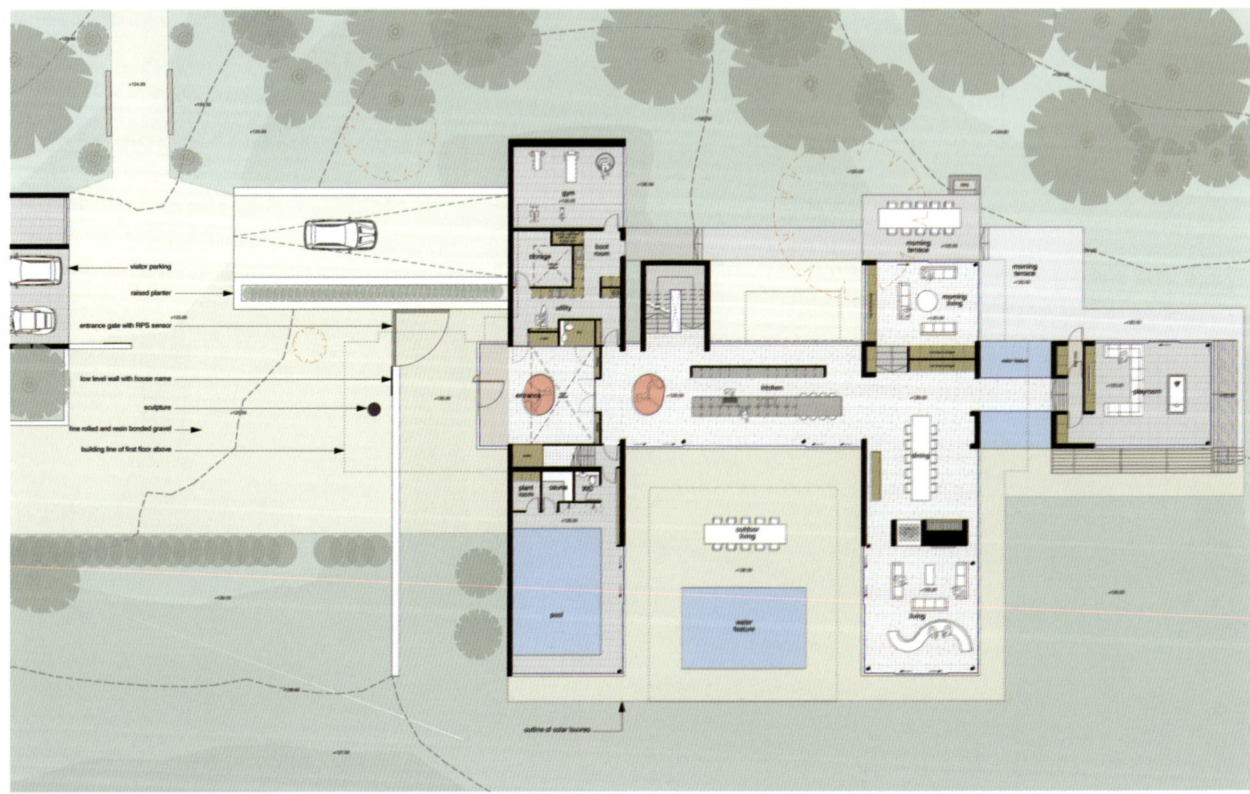

The exterior silhouette is sleek and clearly conceived. Clad in Siberian Larch, patinated green copper and plain copper shingles, the Weber rendered wall panels produce a neutral base that defines the shades, colours and tones of the building mass.

The interior is a chronological progression, a journey through the events of daily life. One parks the car in the linked garage or in front of the house, then proceeds to the fully glazed entrance hall - a grand space that opens up to the kitchen via equally glazed double doors. The kitchen and dining space is in full view from the entrance, with the rest of the house operating in a similar manner; interlinked spaces that flow into one another, accentuating the process of the journey.

Several challenges were posed in the progress of the project. One of the first to arise was the need for planning permission to demolish the existing cottage house. A series of ecology assessments were also undertaken, which resulted in the construction of a 'bat house' as part of the planning condition - the bats living in the existing cottage had to be moved to a new location within the site curtilage.

The resulting home is luxurious and modern, both aesthetically pleasing and sympathetic to the surrounding woodland. The new house provides adequate space for the family, with private bedrooms for each of the three children, and has a number of indulgent features including a sauna, an open shower, a steam room and a gym. The home also boasts a sophisticated automation system, which enables the security, lighting and heating systems to be operated remotely.

Nicolas Tye Architects
The Long Barn Studio,
Limbersey Lane,
Maulden, Bedfordshire MK45 2EA
T: 0152 540 6677
www.nicolastyearchitects.com

Photography: Nerida Howard

SHINGLE HOUSE

Iconic from first glance, this magnificent home set
in the desert terrain of Dungeness is sure to strike
curiosity in even the most imaginative of minds.

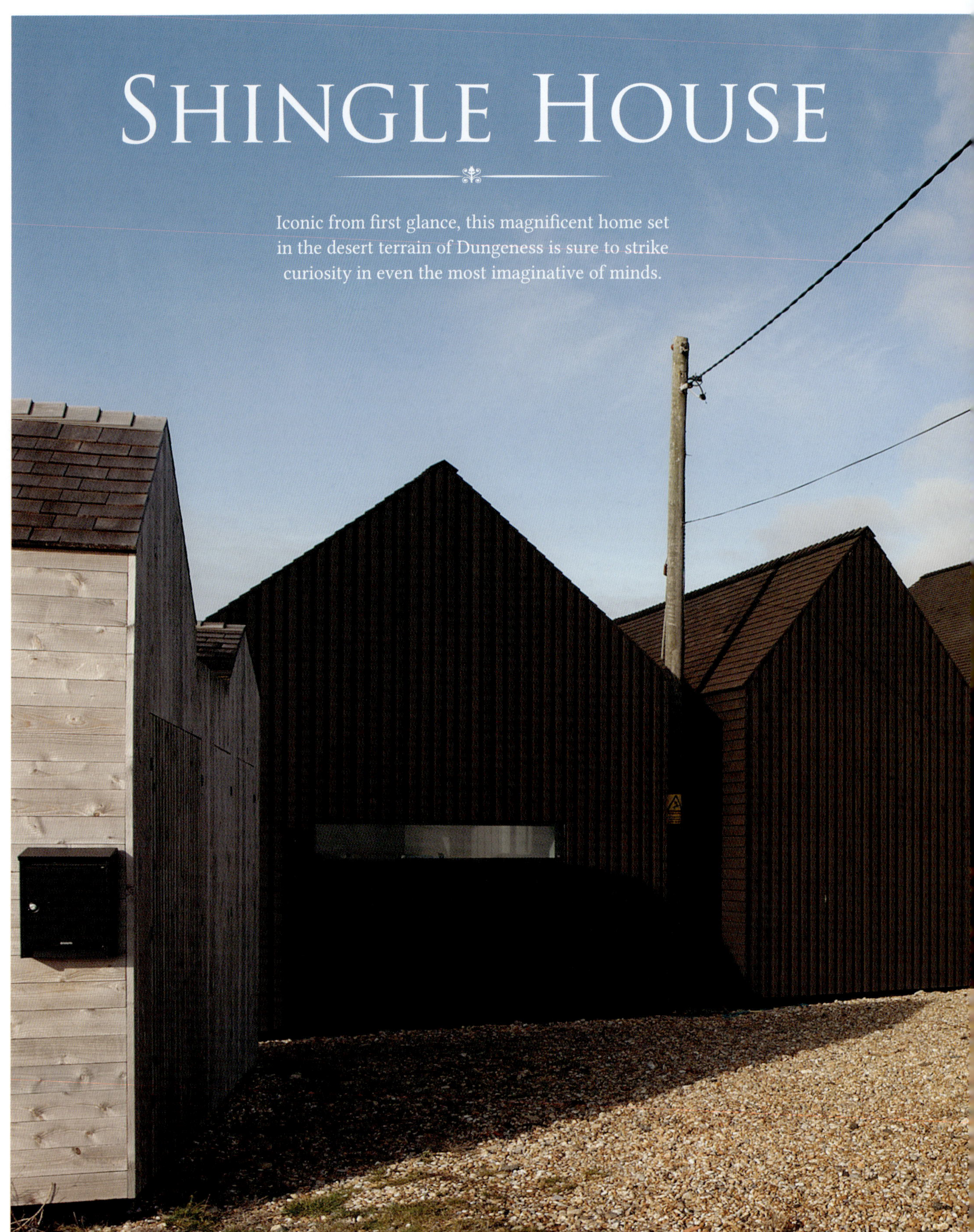

Upper Floor

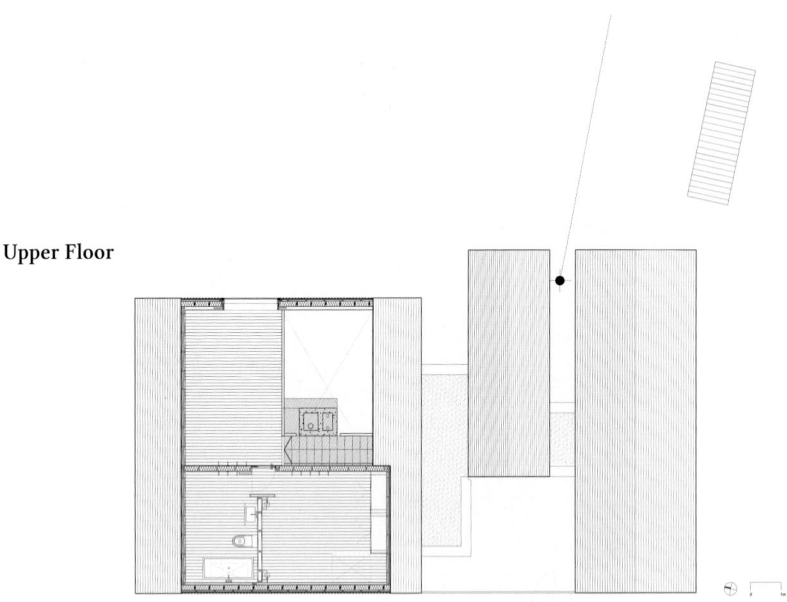

Ground Floor

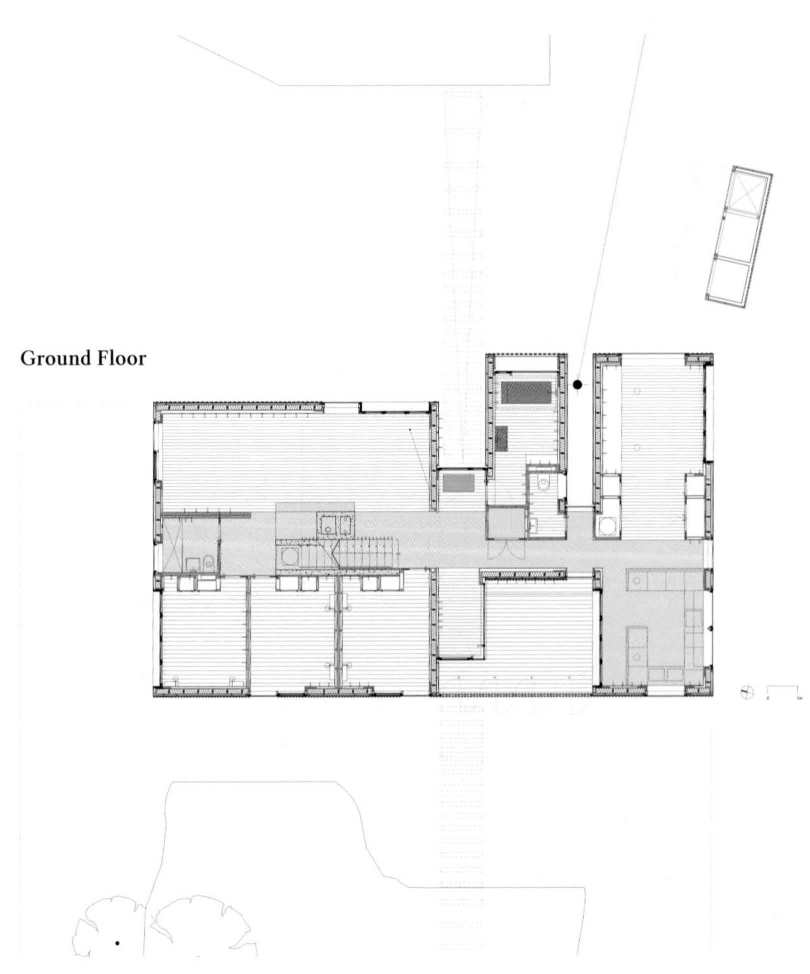

Alan Pert, Director

NORD deliver award-winning architecture and commissioned research into the built environment, taking great inspiration from the UK's legacy of simply 'making things'. This understanding and passion for materials, technological innovation, for detail, craftsmanship, texture and pattern underpins their strong work ethic.

NORD are often provoked and inspired by social and cultural issues, allowing a response in form and materiality. This has led to the development of a series of buildings, places, products and objects, which respond to contemporary needs but celebrate the British tradition of craftsmanship and love of materials.

Nord Architecture
SOUTH BLOCK – Studio 104
Obsorne Street,
Glasgow G1 5QH
T: 0141 552 9996
www.nordarchitecture.com

Cloaked in a 'protective' exoskeleton of tarred timber, the strong black aesthetic provides more than just visual appeal. It provides a functional purpose in the harsh desert environment. Dry winds and salty air are no barrier for the durability of tarred timber, which acts to deflect water and any corrosion associated with the surrounding climate of the shingle wasteland. Punctuated by strange plants and an even more unusual landscape, the building itself fits perfectly within the context of the region.

A remarkably efficient design, this home has the option of opening itself up to views and an interaction with the surrounds, while a unique series of shutters can seal the house off from the drama of the weather, further enhancing the protective skin.

Inside, the home makes use of a refreshing palette. Whites dominate, while a rich timber floor contrasts, adding depth. The ambience is welcoming, with a brightness that vastly contrasts the exterior of the building. It is through a bespoke system of glazing that the penetration of sunlight is afforded, while at the same time, the shape and placement of windows acts as a frame for the gorgeous landscape that lies beyond.

From a central entry point emanates the two 'wings' of the home. To the left, the kitchen and dining area is situated – with a clever fixed bench seat adding to the quirk of the home – along with one bedroom, while the expansive living area and remaining three bedrooms are located to the right.

A central hallway connecting the separate areas of the home acts as a spine that also accommodates the second level of the home. Here, the master bedroom encompasses most of the space, as well as a large en suite and a second living area that appears as a loft from below.

The unique character of this home responds fittingly to the geography of Dungeness and its changing environmental conditions throughout the seasons, while offering a comfortable living solution to those lucky enough to live within.

Photography: Jim Stephenson
(Portrait of Alan Pert by Tim Soar)

HOUSE ON A HILL

❧

House on a Hill is a charming period cottage perched above the North
Sea, Montrose Basin and the Angus Glens. The existing building has
been significantly upgraded, with a large addition, invisible from a
distance, providing generous space for friends, family and children
to interact, all within a modern and comfortable environment.

Nick and Jane Paterson established Paterson Architects in 2004. From their offices in Edinburgh and East Lothian, they work throughout Scotland, endeavouring to bring inspiration and excitement to commissions of any size or type with projects that respect both their surroundings and the environment.

With a goal of "making the ordinary, extraordinary," Paterson Architects offer clients a personal service. Nick and Jane bring their knowledge, experience and creative energy to all projects, each of them having more than fifteen years of previous experience on major projects in the UK, having worked for renowned practices in Glasgow, London and Edinburgh.

Paterson Architects
6 Darnaway Street,
Edinburgh EH3 6BG
T: 0131 220 1088
www.patersonarchitects.com

Respectful of the history of the home, which has been continually occupied for 200 years, the renovation is contextual, site responsive and contemporary, such that it could not have been realised in this form in any other place or time.

Unashamedly modern, this updated cottage and addition is unassuming and robust, sitting comfortably and confidently on its stunning hilltop site. The cottage has been converted to a home office and guest occupation, while the much larger space of the connected extension offers a generous hall and light, flexible family accommodation.

The new and beautiful modern kitchen now forms the heart of the home. It is no longer a detached workplace, but rather a congregation point in which friends and family are entertained. From this central point, the house unfolds in three dimensions, with surrounding space and volume defining circulation and the arrangement of public and private spaces.

The site boasts 360 degree views – a feature that has been thoroughly capitalized upon and can be appreciated from all rooms of the house. The flow of spaces is natural and logical, as there are no doors in the extension to break up the open plan living space. Instead, zones are gently suggested by variations in the floor level and ceiling height - a more subtle demarcation of space. Oak has been used throughout the design as a warm and unifying design element across the flooring and some items of furniture.

Corner windows subvert the introverted nature of the simple and appropriately scaled volumes, tracking the sun and opening the interior to the landscape and horizon beyond. The timber cladding utilised on the exterior fades into the landscape when viewed against the white render of the existing cottage, thus ensuring that the beautiful historic façade is what takes centre stage when approaching the home. As a result, the extension does not dominate the existing space and the new parapet height keeps the profile well below the existing ridge.

Simple, restrained and relaxed, the design of this home aimed for 'good ordinariness' - a pragmatic approach driven both by the clients' brief and the opportunities presented by the site, and developed without formal agenda or polemic. The house is not luxurious, but in accordance with Paterson Architects' mission statement, it does make the ordinary extraordinary, sacrificing extravagant and willful design for a practical and purposeful aesthetic.

Photography: Keith Hunter Photography

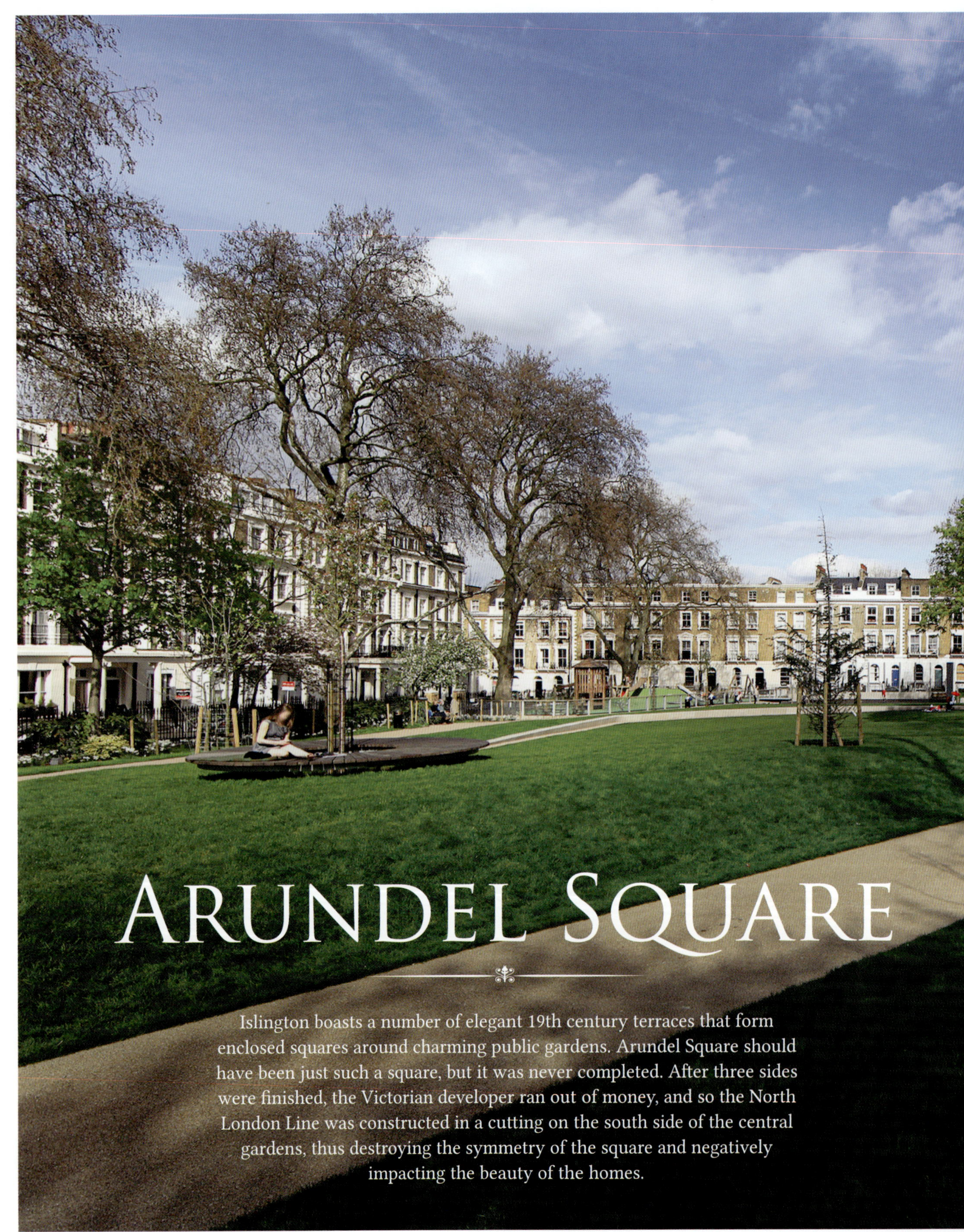

Arundel Square

Islington boasts a number of elegant 19th century terraces that form
enclosed squares around charming public gardens. Arundel Square should
have been just such a square, but it was never completed. After three sides
were finished, the Victorian developer ran out of money, and so the North
London Line was constructed in a cutting on the south side of the central
gardens, thus destroying the symmetry of the square and negatively
impacting the beauty of the homes.

© Tim Crocker

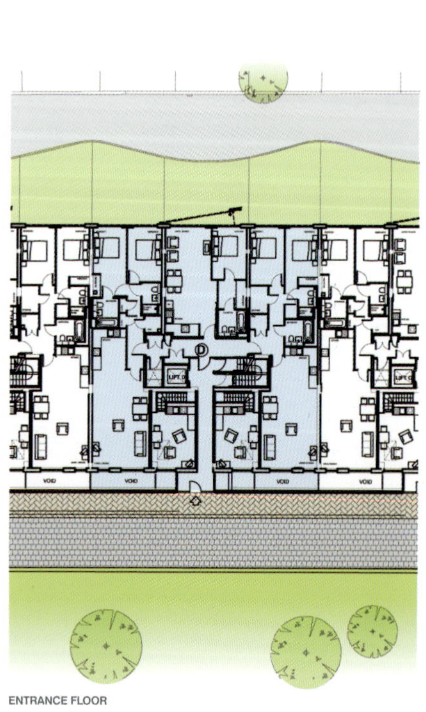

ENTRANCE FLOOR

TYPICAL FLOOR

Andrew Beharrell

Teresa Borsuk

Stephen Fisher

Pollard Thomas Edwards architects (PTEa) specialise in the creation of new neighbourhoods and the revitalisation of old ones. Executive Directors Andrew Beharrell, Stephen Fisher and Teresa Borsuk all share years of experience and a commitment to producing innovative responses to sites and client requirements.

PTEa offers a unique combination of commercial acumen, design talent and social commitment. Their rigorous, questioning approach produces solutions that are both intelligent and imaginative, adding value and joy to each of their designs. Working closely and collaboratively with their clients, they forge long-term relationships, placing great importance not only on the way buildings look, but on how they are made, the way they are used and the grace of their ageing.

PTEa - Pollard Thomas Edwards architects
Diespeker Wharf,
38 Graham Street,
London N1 8JX
T: 0207 336 7777
www.ptea.co.uk

After 150 years of life in this unfortunate state, Pollard Thomas Edwards architects have successfully completed the space by adding the missing fourth side of housing. They began with the radical idea of decking over the cutting, creating an extra acre of land. The project took decades to complete, but the results speak for themselves in the now stunning family-friendly space, transformed from a sparsely inhabited and depressing area to a charming public garden.

Rather than blindly construct a pastiche of the beautiful Victorian buildings that line three sides of the square, the new building is a contemporary apartment scheme for mixed tenure, which draws on the scale and intricacy of the existing buildings, but reinterprets these elements in a modern, functional and aesthetically charming way.

The six-storey block has a limestone framework with projecting balconies and a largely glazed façade. The new building provides 147 mixed-tenure apartments that are based around multiple cores in order to give most flats a dual aspect. In particular, the fifth-floor penthouses were conceived and planned to take full advantage of views across and into the public gardens. Additionally, these living spaces have fully-glazed elevations to the square, with bedrooms at the rear.

In contrast to the appearance of the square-facing façade, the rear is composed predominately of brick, much like the rear of the Victorian buildings, and features aluminium and glass oriel windows in addition to vertical banks of balconies with Iroko timber screens.

Client: Londonewcastle and United House Developments
Photography: Tim Crocker, SJA Photography and Rejash Bhela

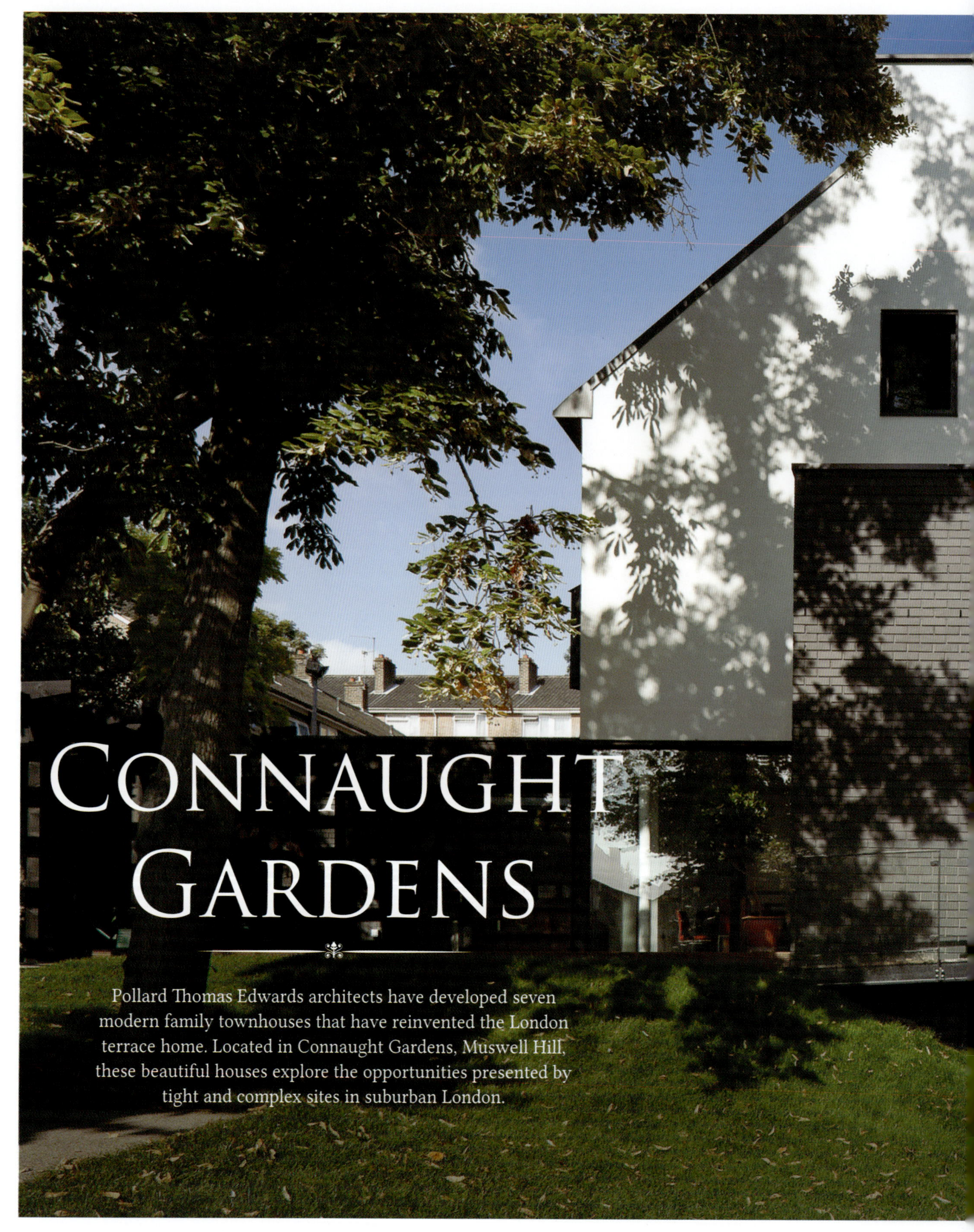

CONNAUGHT GARDENS

Pollard Thomas Edwards architects have developed seven modern family townhouses that have reinvented the London terrace home. Located in Connaught Gardens, Muswell Hill, these beautiful houses explore the opportunities presented by tight and complex sites in suburban London.

© Tim Crocker

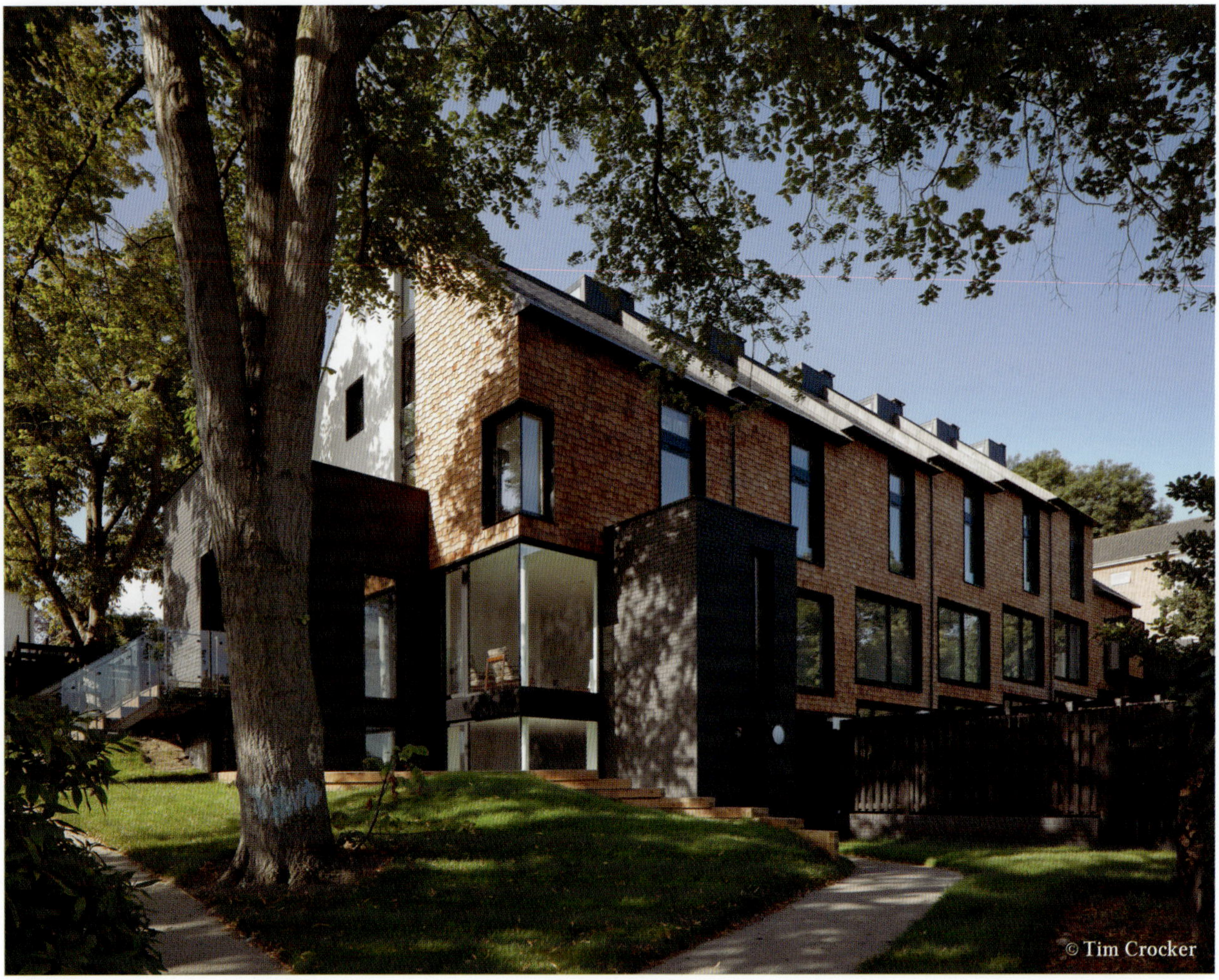

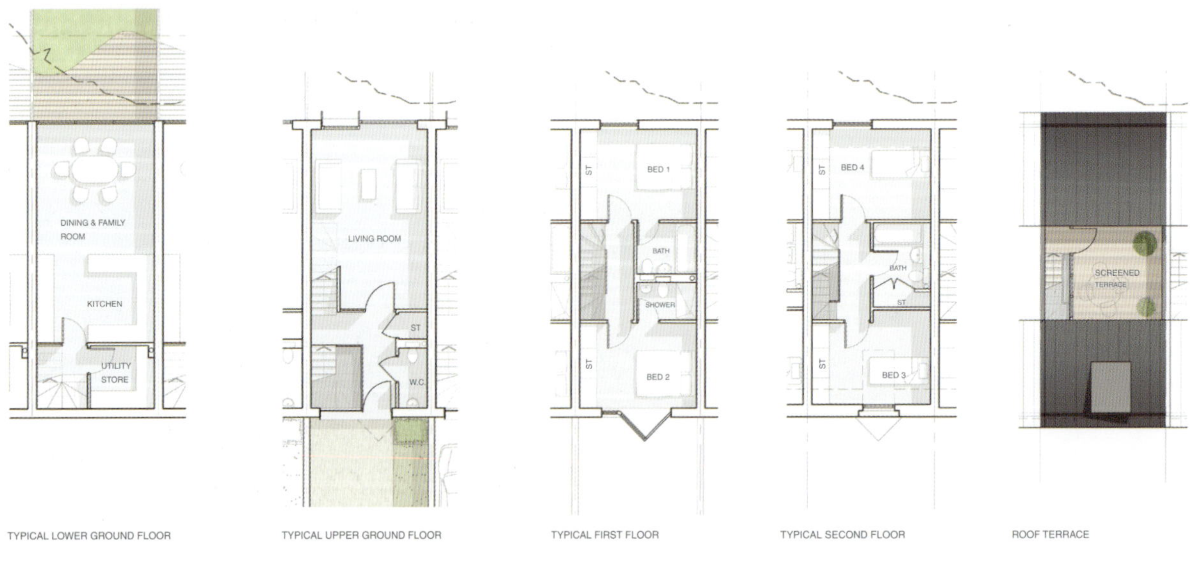

TYPICAL LOWER GROUND FLOOR

TYPICAL UPPER GROUND FLOOR

TYPICAL FIRST FLOOR

TYPICAL SECOND FLOOR

ROOF TERRACE

METRES
0 1 2 3 4 5

TYPICAL HOUSE PLANS

© Tim Crocker

© Tim Crocker

The site, located on a private lane, was previously occupied by a single derelict house in a large wooded garden. This garden contained five protected trees, which added a constraining factor to the potential development. In addition, the site has a steep slope in two directions, and so an economical construction method was devised to cope with this. A folded concrete basement on piled foundations now steps down the site, anchored by three load bearing masonry volumes.

The façade is characterised by the use of traditional materials that are applied with contemporary detail in a modern suburban vernacular. The terrace, when approached from the north, is faced with cedar shingles that give a layered appearance reminiscent of tree-bark, thus merging the structure naturally with the wooded context around it. The pitched roof disguises a terrace, which sits within the ridge line and forms an entirely private space, one large enough for an outdoor table with chairs, some sun lounges, or even a vegetable garden; a charming secret roof terrace with a stunning view of the London skyline and a panorama of treetops crowned by Alexandra Palace.

The southern elevation contrasts with the northern façade, relating to the black and white Tudor-bethan style of the immediate neighbours. The crisp white cladding is punctuated by black zinc 'seams', a modern take on the traditional style.

Designed with economic and efficient operation in mind, each home requires only the minimum of energy input to achieve a level of temperature comfort. Underfloor heating and whole-house ventilation act in combination with a high performance envelope to ensure that climate control is straightforward. Additionally, the staircase, located at the centre of the house, concludes in a glazed rooftop lantern. Solar gain from this lantern creates a passive stack chimney, drawing warm air from the adjoining rooms below and replacing it with cooler air from the windows opening to the perimeter. The continuous effect this has, in combination with the house-wide ventilation, provides cooling to the house in peak summer temperatures.

The inside spaces are simple and modern, creating a neutral, yet dynamic backdrop for modern family living. Living areas have wall-to-wall glazing, while white ceramic tile flooring reflects light deep into the home and adds a clean internal decoration. Though this flooring option may appear cold to the touch, the underfloor heating systems serve to keep the tiled surfaces at a pleasant temperature.

Though the houses are in fact four storeys high, they appear to be only three due to the inclusion of attic bedrooms. Within each home there are two bedroom floors, offering four bedrooms in total. This extra floor is disguised with clerestory windows, which at street level seem to be merely a continuation of the windows on the floor below, but in reality are situated at floor level inside.

PTEa - Pollard Thomas Edwards architects
Dicspeker Wharf,
38 Graham Street,
London N1 8JX
T: 0207 336 7777
www.ptea.co.uk

Client: Connaught House Developments
(a joint venture between PTE Property and Guild Developments)
Photography: Tim Crocker

GUNPOWDER MILL

These magnificent 19th century buildings located on a site of historical importance have been respectfully converted into a flexible and expansive office space, remaining faithful to the industrial history of the site while adding a contemporary twist. A new three-storey glazed structure forms a link between the two existing buildings, providing magnificent views over the adjacent water meadows and completing the new headquarters.

© Rejash Bhela

© Justin Laskin

© Dennis Gilbert / VIEW

© Dennis Gilbert / VIEW

© Justin Laskin

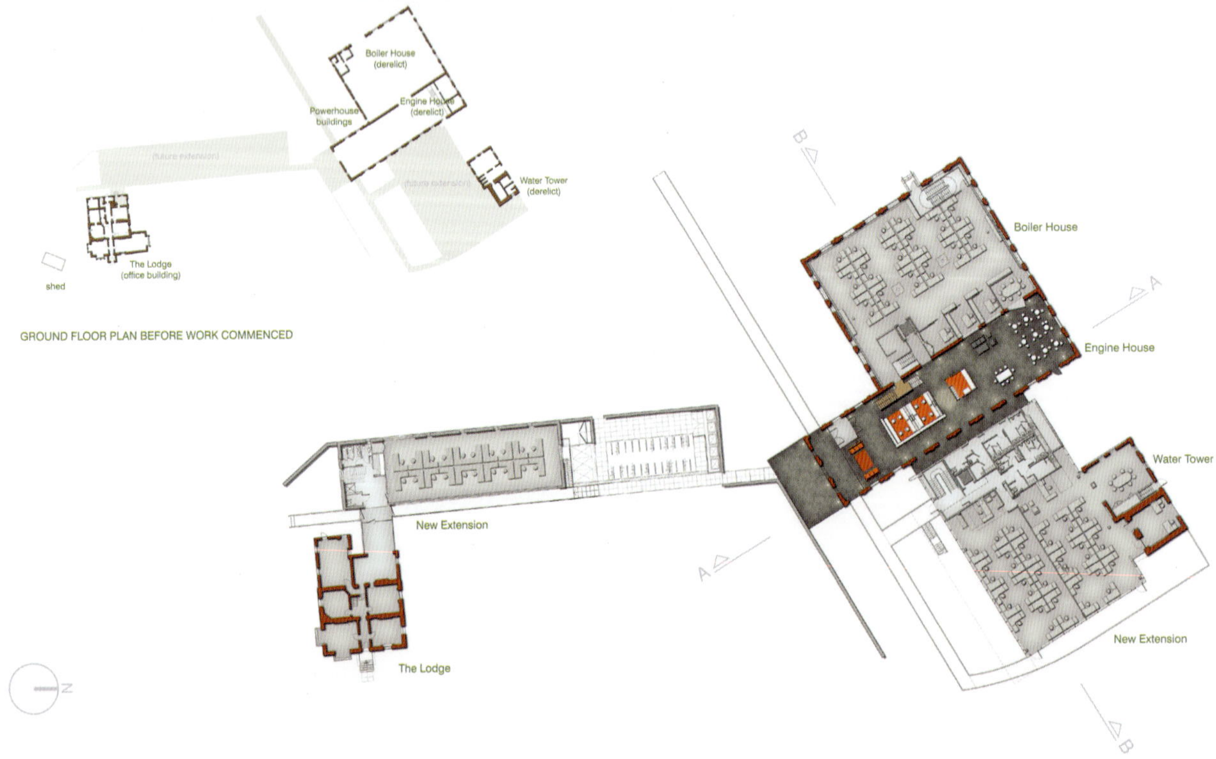
Boiler House
(derelict)
Powerhouse
buildings
Engine House
(derelict)
Water Tower
(derelict)
The Lodge
(office building)
shed
GROUND FLOOR PLAN BEFORE WORK COMMENCED
New Extension
The Lodge
N
Boiler House
Engine House
Water Tower
New Extension

The project aimed to convert, refurbish and extend the aging industrial listed buildings in a way that would suit the current practices and future plans for a growing company. Thanks to careful planning and inspired design, the resulting modern office environment will evolve in line with the owners, offering new and flexible solutions as the needs for the space grow and change.

Lying on the outskirts of London, adjacent to a river and surrounded by natural woodland, substantial work was required to repair and restore the fabric of the building. Despite this, the culture of the conversion strictly adhered to sensitive restoration with a light and gentle touch. The result preserves the historical significance of the site, which was once the largest gunpowder works in Britain.

The old power house and water tower have been converted to form the new headquarters of the client company. One of the 3-bay buildings was kept at a single volume, creating a conceptual heart for the new design and a place of arrival, connection and meeting. The new three-storey glass structure is a light-flooded modern addition that forms both a physical link between the buildings and a strong conceptual link between the old and new elements of the structure.

The new steelwork is plainly visible, producing a materialistic gesture to the simpler detailing of traditional industrial buildings. The new and old steelwork are expressed in two colours, with the new interventions remaining subservient to the older spaces. Planar glass is used to bring light into the area and is carefully cut into existing brickwork.

New internal finishes to the offices reflect a contemporary environment while subtle references are retained, drawing the original industrial fabric into the new design, such as that seen in the exposed brick window arches. The custom Corian reception desk and bespoke feature light wall and signage bring a touch of something decadent to the otherwise restrained, practical space.

Client: Gunpowder Mill Developments Ltd.
Photography: Rejash Bhela, Darren Chung, Justin Laskin and Dennis Gilbert

PTEa - Pollard Thomas Edwards architects
Diespeker Wharf,
38 Graham Street,
London N1 8JX
T: 0207 336 7777
www.ptea.co.uk

FURZEY HALL FARM

This is a home in which form and function work in unison with a blend of old and new styles to create a beautiful living space. Unassuming from the exterior, the new aspects of the home almost go unnoticed.

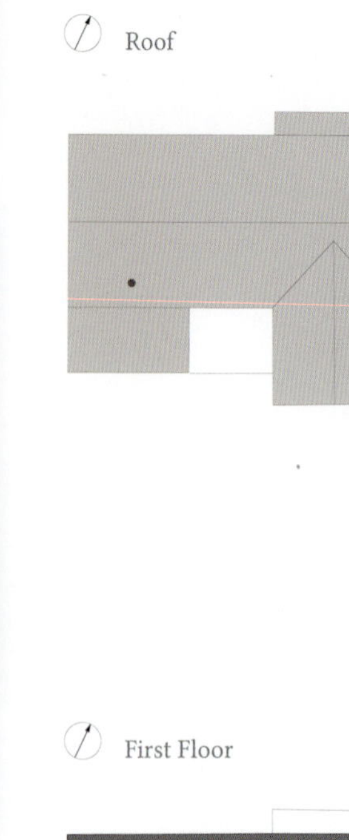

First Floor

Ground Floor
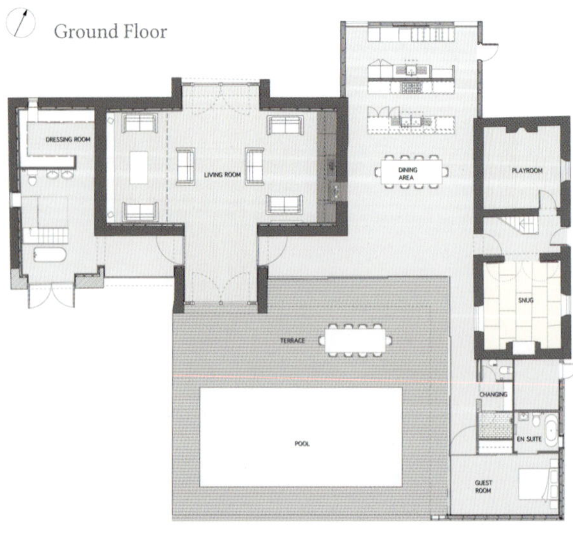

Andrew Waugh is a founding director of Waugh Thistleton Architects, established in 1997 with Anthony Thistleton. Andrew is passionate about architecture. Over the last 15 years, the practice has worked hard on award winning schemes from cinemas to synagogues, social housing to shopping centres. Respected for both public and private buildings, Waugh Thistleton have a wealth and breadth of experience. Andrew is a dedicated advocate of timber construction, and in 2010 was awarded the RIBA president's medal for research.

In addition to lecturing all over the world on architecture and construction, Andrew has taught at many Universities from Yale to Cambridge and is an external examiner for the University of East London and practice tutor at Greenwich. Andrew is an enthusiastic Hackney resident and a chair of the council's design panel.

Waugh Thistleton Architects
74 Paul Street,
London EC2A 4NA
T: 0207 613 5727
www.waughthistleton.com

Burned timber works perfectly with the cobbled and charming façade of the original building, with strong lines that lead the eye from one end of the property to the other. Affirming an historic air from the outside, the weathered shell protects a sharply contrasted modern interior.

From anywhere in the home, it is possible to feel a distinct connection with the outdoors. Full length glazing in the dining room really makes this home one of discussion. An impressive amount of light is also let into the house, helping to maintain a comfortable temperature through the inclusion of clerestory windows to maximize solar gain.

However, some of the greatest features of this home are not aesthetic, or even visible for that matter. Site orientation is key to the practicality of the design, allowing for greater views and a better relationship with the surrounding environment. In addition, sustainable features such as solar panels for power and ground source heat pumps that warm the home in winter. The exceptional slate-lined swimming pool to the rear of the property has its water drawn from a well, filtering through reeds to create a pragmatic feature to an already astounding home.

Back inside, Puur concrete flooring is a gorgeous contrast to the texture of the existing Cotswold stone walls. The bathrooms are a welcome curio, melding industrial coldness in glass and steel with the allure of antique fittings.

Fascinating from the inside out, it's almost impossible to overlook this magnificent amalgamation of old and new.

Photography: Will Pryce

THE WHITE HOUSE

Hard and soft surfaces as well as geometric and organic form work
together here with unmatched coherence in paying homage to the
roots of this home that stretch as far back as the mid 1700s.

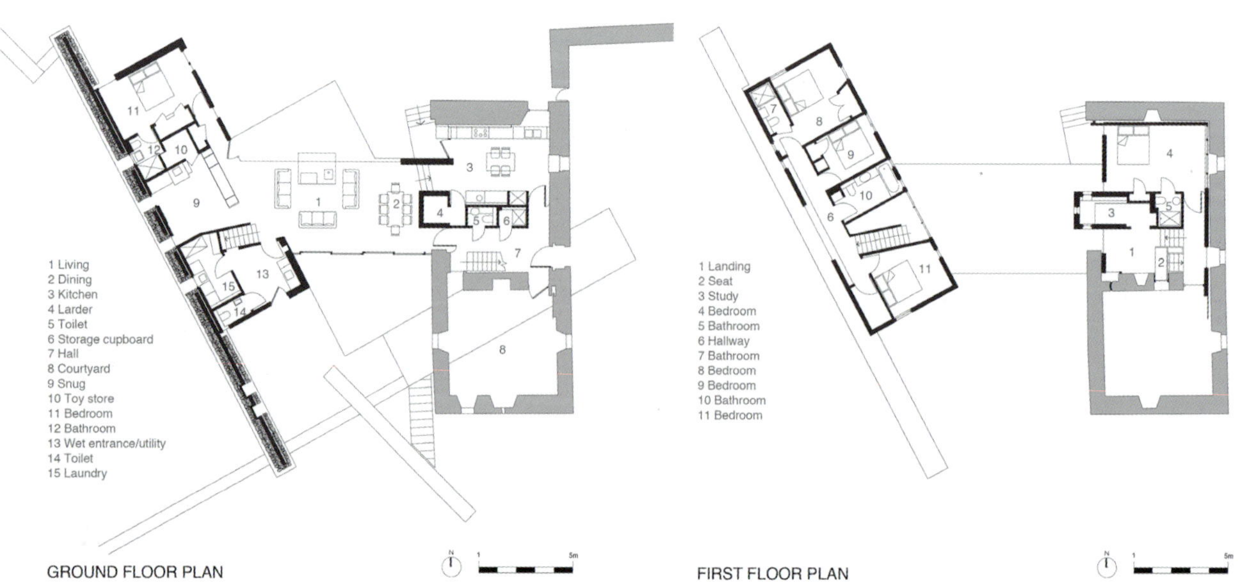

GROUND FLOOR PLAN

FIRST FLOOR PLAN

WTArchitecture was formed in 2005 by architect William Tunnell. The practice's work has focused on contemporary interventions in historic buildings and contexts, and on responsive landscape buildings, often in sensitive and dramatic locations. William Tunnell trained in Bath before working with Richard Murphy's highly successful practice in Edinburgh and tutoring at Edinburgh University. WTArchitecture's reputation for delivering high quality contextual architecture has led to further commissions for both private houses and community buildings across Scotland, and in particular in the Highlands and the Hebrides.

Interestingly enough, it was the first lime-built, square-cornered home in the area and served as a site of leisure and entertainment for Boswell and Johnston in 1773 whilst stormbound during their famous tour of Scotland.

Sympathetic to its heritage, WT Architecture have utilised a curious mix of materials that not only highlight the building, but allow its additions to fit in seamlessly with the original lime structure. The juxtaposition of glass and stone, with timber and tiling create a stunning effect, entwining vintage character with modern class. A flow between spaces is afforded due to the airy feel of the abode. Quaint from the outside but unassumingly spacious inside, there is plenty of room for a growing family.

A masonry wall constructed of locally sourced stone protects the home from the prevailing westerly winds, allowing the home to be oriented toward Grishipol Bay and views to the northeast. Aside from its functional intention, this orientation also ensures that the original historic structure retains a higher profile as seen from the nearby road and from the bay itself.

The project as a whole is intended to appear as though the spaces overlap, although it is through the careful selection of materials that a differentiation between each important element of the home is realised. Establishing a strong series of connecting spaces whilst preserving the individual identity of each element, the home offers a unique style that encapsulates the surrounding environment and in return, is enhanced by the drama of its rugged coastal location.

A holistic approach to sustainability has been taken throughout this project, noting nuances of sociological and environmental sustainability through design, procurement, construction and operation. Also central to the design is its emphasis on longevity. Materials used and the layout chosen all allow for a lifetime of occupancy and maximisation of use in outdoor areas.

Photography: Andrew Lee

WTArchitecture
4-6 Gote Lane,
South Queensferry,
Edinburgh, EH30 9PS
T: 0131 331 2813
www.wtarchitecture.com

Designer: Nicolas Tye Architects
Project: The Long Barn
Photograph provided by Nicolas Tye Architects

Designer: David Mikhail Architects
Project: Hoxton
Photographer: Tim Crocker

Designer: Architecture:m Chartered Architects
Project: Regent Road
Photographer: Andrew Haslam

Designer: Nicolas Tye Architects
Project: Rammamera
Photographer: Nerida Howard

Designer: Nicolas Tye Architects
Project: Cedarwood
Photograph provided by Nicolas Tye Architects

Designer: Architecture:m Chartered Architects
Project: Regent Road
Photographer: Andrew Haslam